"I've spent 15 years in senior PR an
with blue chip companies and can.
doesn't know about communications, isn't worth knowing!! He's a true genius and his advice is indispensable."

Helen Mills, Global PR Director, AstraZeneca

"Andy Bounds taught me more about effective presenting
than a lady who'd previously taught two US Presidents."

**Drayton Bird, Chairman of Drayton Bird Partnership
and world leading authority on direct marketing**

"Andy's techniques are so effective yet simple to apply, that
they are bordering on genius."

**Sue Aldridge, Business Development Manager, Royal
Bank of Scotland**

"Andy Bounds has a totally unique and inspiring way of
communicating. He also has this tremendous ability to help
others achieve more when they communicate. Every single
person he's worked with at npower has found his guidance
to be immensely valuable, and to have made a real difference. My advice: read this book – it will help you communicate with, and relate to, people better than ever before."

Heidi Walton, People Development Manager, npower

"I know the critical moment which changed our business
was when we started working with Andy Bounds. Since that
time, we've completed a row of major pitches to prospects
and we've won them all, including the New Zealand Government...."

Mark Sinclair, Managing Director, Hubbub (UK) Ltd

"They say the definition of genius is the ability to make the complex simple. If that's the case then Andy Bounds is a genius. Right now you hold in your a hand a book packed with insight and ideas that makes the whole art of communication and connecting with people both easy to understand and apply. Yes, you'll have the occasional B.F.O.(Blinding Flash of the Obvious) moment and wonder why on earth you've never thought of some of the ideas before...... truth is we need some one like Andy with his incredibly easy style of writing to wake us up to the obvious. I defy anyone who reads this book and applies the insights to their own business not to see a increase in both their profit and their profile."

Paul McGee, International speaker and best selling author of *S.U.M.O. (Shut Up, Move On)*

"I have found training and advice from Andy Bounds to have been a real benefit, the proof of the pudding being in some fantastic recent results from presentations to FTSE 250 companies."

David Hunt, Corporate Fundraiser, Barnardo's

"Basically get speaking with Andy Bounds if you want success whatever you may be doing."

Ian Martin, Area Premier development Manager, HSBC

"There are absolutely no doubts in our minds now that hiring Andy Bounds is going to prove one of the most effective investments we have ever made in our business."

Gillian & Martin Lawson, European Directors, Business Networking International

"After Andy had finished with us, our sales began to rocket. We weren't pushing people into signing up. As if by magic, prospective clients were signing up with us WITHOUT us using traditional 'closing' techniques. Anyone who puts off engaging Andy Bounds will certainly miss out on an opportunity."

Ian Denny, Managing Director, CHT Solutions Ltd

"I wish I had met him sooner."

Sarah Owen, Managing Director, The Referral Institute UK

The Jelly Effect

How to make your communication stick

ANDY BOUNDS

CAPSTONE

First published 2007 by:
Capstone Publishing Ltd. (a Wiley Company)
The Atrium, Southern Gate, Chichester, PO19 8SQ, UK.
www.wileyeurope.com
Email (for orders and customer service enquires): cs-books@wiley.co.uk

Reprinted June 2007

Other Wiley Editorial Offices
John Wiley & Sons Inc., 111 River Street, Hoboken, NJ 07030, USA
Jossey-Bass, 989 Market Street, San Francisco, CA 94103–1741, USA
Wiley-VCH Verlag GmbH, Boschstr. 12, D-69469 Weinheim, Germany
John Wiley & Sons Australia Ltd, 42 McDougall Street, Milton, Queensland 4064, Australia
John Wiley & Sons (Asia) Pte Ltd, 2 Clementi Loop #02–01, Jin Xing Distripark, Singapore
129809
John Wiley & Sons Canada Ltd, 22 Worcester Road, Etobicoke, Ontario, Canada M9W 1L1
Wiley also publishes its books in a variety of electronic formats. Some content that appears in
print may not be available in electronic books.

Library of Congress Cataloging-in-Publication Data

Bounds, Andy.
  The jelly effect : making your communication stick / by Andy Bounds.
    p. cm.
  Includes bibliographical references and index.
  ISBN 978-1-84112-760-6 (pbk. : alk. paper)
  1. Business communication. I. Title.
  HF5718.B658 2007
  658.4'5--dc22

                                                                    2006100403

Anniversary Logo Design: Richard J. Pacifico

Set in ITC New Baskerville by Sparks (www.sparks.co.uk)
Printed and bound in Great Britain by TJ International Ltd, Padstow, Cornwall

To my children Megan and Jack.
I love you both very much.

Contents

Acknowledgements

It all started last year …

A great friend of mine, fellow professional speaker Paul McGee, introduced me to John Moseley and Iain Campbell from his publishers Capstone. John, Iain and I hit it off straight away, all sharing a real passion for personal development, and decided to create this book together. They've given me invaluable guidance and support throughout the entire process, and I'm delighted to be associated with them and their company.

But, even with Paul, John and Iain's support, this book would never have happened if it had been left to me to type it (I'm pretty sure I'm the slowest typist who's ever lived). So, a huge thank you goes to my two highly-skilled and very patient typists: Jayne Smith of Document Direct, and my mother Geraldine, for the hundreds of hours of work they did.

Talking of my mother, as you will see from reading this book, she and my Father (Peter) have been a huge inspiration to me in everything I do. I am really proud of, and grateful to, them both.

Also, a big thank you must go to Sarah, Liz and all my colleagues for everything they do to make our business such a success.

And finally, the biggest thanks of all go to Emma, my editor, best friend, fiancée, business partner, sounding-board and soul mate. Em, this book – like everything else in my life – wouldn't have worked without you.

Who am I to tell you how to communicate?

I have always had very poor eyesight.

I'm blind in one eye. My 'good' eye has a prescription of -14.5 (hardly anybody is less than -10) which means – amongst other things – I can't see far enough to drive. And at school I always had to sit at the front to see properly.

Also, you won't be surprised to know, I don't judge distances very well. I'm not very good at catching things. I can't make out those 'magic eye' pictures. And the only thing 3D glasses do for me is keep everything 2D, but turn it red.

Yet, bizarrely enough, my bad eyesight has given me an incredibly powerful insight into how to communicate in business – and I wager you won't have come across it anywhere else.

Let me explain …

You see, to me, business communication has to do only one thing. It doesn't have to entertain, impress or astonish. It just has to *work*. To achieve what you want it to. A good sales pitch gets the sale. A great motivational speaker motivates. A successful training workshop improves delegates' performance.

Well, my eyesight has helped me show thousands of businesses how to make their communications do what they're supposed to do: be infinitely more effective.

For instance, one client – a major bank – won business from 18 sales pitches out of 18 after working with me.

Another client was already a very successful international speaker, motivator and marketing legend. He said after our first meeting, which lasted less than an hour, that I had taught him *more about effective presenting than a lady who had previously taught two American Presidents*.

I've helped TV personalities, blue-chip firms, industry leaders, business experts, national charities, sales teams, politicians achieve more when communicating … all, believe it or not, because I'm quite literally 'half-blind'.

But how does this make me more able to help people communicate?

Well, you see my sight is a symptom of a hereditary condition called Stickler's Syndrome. I have it. My daughter Megan has it. And my mother has it.

In fact, my mother is totally blind. She lost her sight when she was eight (about the same age as I lost the sight in my left eye). Her blindness led to me having to do things – and explain things – others never have to.

As a child, I would sit on my mother's knee and ask her, 'What's the best way to describe this room to you, Mum? How can I explain it so you understand it *instantly*?' And I used to have these conversations with her about every subject imaginable – people, images, landscapes, rooms she hadn't been in before, describing films so she could enjoy them as much as a sighted person could, and so on.

So, for as long as I can remember, I have known something very few other people anywhere truly know: that *the natural way you speak is not the natural way for somebody else to understand.* I had to change the way I described things, how I put them in context, so Mum could easily understand, benefit from and – most importantly – act on what I said.

Now, you may well be thinking, 'How does Andy talking to his blind mother have any relevance to me? I don't tend to come across blind people in business very much.'

And I'm sure you don't. But:

- Have you ever been bored during someone's presentation? It would be amazing if you haven't: a staggering 97% of managers find it hard to stay awake in presentations. Main reasons include too much information, overly long presentations and reading from slides – Research by PTP Training and Marketing.
- Ever been in a meeting where you could have walked out half way through without it making any difference to your life whatsoever?
- Ever had a tedious, pointless conversation when you've been networking?
- Ever failed to win a piece of business that, deep down, you know you could/should have won?

I bet you have. Everybody has. But one day I found a way of applying what I learned when talking to my mother to everyday business communications – like networking, presenting, training, meetings, interviews – which is totally new and astoundingly effective.

You see, my mother is very clever. Consider how long the legal profession has existed in the UK – literally hundreds of years. And she's only the second blind British female solicitor ever.

So although she's very intelligent, she just happens not to see. And, when you speak to others in business, they too may well be very bright. But they may not see things from your point of view.

So, you need to put things in context for them. Just like I had to – and still do – for my mother.

And that's what this book is all about. I'm going to show you how to get the results you want when speaking to others. Whether they're groups or individuals. Whether formally or informally. Whether inside or outside your organization.

In other words, this book will help you achieve more from your verbal communication than ever before.

You see, the common denominator with every type of communication is there is an audience. And, if you put things from their point of view, you have a much better chance of success.

Now, I know you already know that, but you're about to learn what I realized at a very early age: that, despite knowing this, very few people truly communicate from the audience's viewpoint. Even if they think they are doing. And this is the simple, overwhelmingly important reason why they don't achieve what they want.

So, this book will show you how to impress anyone when you first meet them by saying the right things in the right way. Similarly, you'll discover the easiest, quickest way to sell anything to anyone. You'll learn how to ask people who know, like and trust you to recommend you to others. And you'll learn a simple technique to achieve what you want from your presentations.

You'll see that – to achieve all these things – all you need is a change in the emphasis of what you say, a tweaking of the order in which you say it, minor adjustments to standard phrases that you use, and your results will rocket. By the time you finish this book, you will know exactly what to say – and how to say it – to enjoy far greater levels of success.

As a final – and very important – point, I guess you don't have a great deal of free time. Nobody does any more, do they? So, this book has been written and designed with that in mind.

Have a look at the next chapter, 'The best way for you to read this book', to see how you can get the most value from it in the shortest possible time, and start learning some new, incredibly simple and very powerful ways to impress, motivate and persuade more people when you speak to them.

Andy Bounds

The best way for you to read this book

I'm lazy. That's why I read lots of business books.

Drayton Bird

I once heard Drayton Bird make a surprising confession.

'I'm lazy,' he said. 'That's why I read lots of business books.'

This sounded very strange to me. 'Why would someone lazy bother reading books?' I asked him.

His reply made perfect sense, though.

'Most people waste half their lives *guessing* what will work. They try, fail, and squander time and money for years making it up as they go along. Why guess when you can know from someone who's done it all before?

'I can spend a day reading a book, do exactly what it tells me, and get it right first time. That's why I'm lazy. I'd rather do one day's good work than twenty years of bad.'

BRILLIANT BUSINESS BOOKS

This made a lot of sense to me, though I'm not too sure I'd like to call myself *lazy*. I like *time-efficient* better.

But it's not only *time-efficiency* I look for when I read business books. I want them to have the following attributes:

1   Most important: give me tips that are *all*:
    • new (that I haven't heard before);
    • simple (so they are painless for me to implement);
    • relevant (so I can apply them to my business);
    • accessible (so I can understand them and put them to work easily); and
    • effective (i.e. they *work*).
2   The book must help me to be *time-efficient* when reading it. This could mean teaching me lots of things in a short space of time, or being clearly signposted so I can easily find the things that matter most to me.

Are you like me? Do you want *this* book to do those things for you? I hope so. Because I have written the book assuming you do. And here's how …

Attribute 1 – New, simple, relevant, accessible and effective tips
Every tip, hint or technique in this book has been carefully selected to be:

• *New* – either my unique way of looking at things, or presenting in a new way the results of years of study into what persuades and stays in the memory.
• *Simple* – one of my clients once said I give 'annoyingly simple advice'. In his words: 'I could have thought of every single thing you said, but never have. Nor has anybody else I've ever met.'

Everything in this book is easy for you to incorporate into your standard way of working, and is fast-acting.

- *Relevant* – unless yours is a strange kind of business I've never come across, everything in this book should apply to what you need to sell or persuade others about.
- *Accessible* – throughout the book, you'll find lots of simple exercises so you can apply what I have said to your own business, to make sure this book becomes a practical guide, rather than a theoretical manual.
- *Effective* – everything you read in this book *works*. It has been tested by the thousands of businesses I have worked with, so I know what happens when people implement the advice you're about to get.

Attribute 2 – Time-efficient
This book is easy to read time-efficiently.

If you like to read cover to cover, this book takes you on a journey. I start by showing you how to have far greater impact and get better results when you speak to strangers (at networking events) … building up to how to present to groups, again with greater impact, and better results.

However, if you have a more targeted, selective approach to reading – would rather zero in on what matters to you – I've ensured each section is totally self-contained, making complete sense on its own. That way, for example, if you only want to know how to be better at networking, simply read Section 4.

But, however you read this book, to make sure you get the best out of it, there are two sections you must read …

Getting going ...

If you're planning to dip in and out of relevant sections, turn to the Contents on page ix and see where you want to go first. To remind you, all the sections are self-contained, so you can read them in any order.

However, the two sections you simply must read for this book to get you the best results are:

- **Section 2: *Why 'the Jelly Effect?'*** – This section explains the single biggest problem in business communications (as well as shedding light on the title of this book).
- **Section 3: *The AFTERs*** – Of everything that I have ever taught any business person anywhere, the thing that has had the biggest impact on their success is the 'AFTERs', which is a process I've developed to make communication more powerful. Because AFTERs are so fundamental to business communication and all the subsequent sections keep referring to them, the book won't make sense unless you read this section.

These sections won't take long to read, but give you an instant appreciation of what you need to do to get better results every time you speak to others.

Why 'the Jelly Effect'?

How many times have you been excruciatingly bored when listening to a presentation?

How many times have you been itching to get away from someone at a networking event, as they drone on and on?

How many times have you been aggressively sold-to and thought, 'I'd rather be somewhere else … anywhere else. Just *not* here.'

I'll bet it's hundreds of times. It certainly is with me. And with every person I've ever asked these questions to.

But, what about the other way around… when it's *you* who's presenting, who's networking, who's selling?

Do you ever bore people to death? Do you drone on when you should shut up? Do you sell in a way that comes over as too aggressive?

Have you ever felt that sickening feeling when presenting: 'Oh no, I'm losing the audience … they look so bored … they're looking round the room … they're fidgeting … and I've still got 10 minutes to go … I'll speed up and get it over'?

When networking, have you ever seen the person you're speaking to constantly glance over your shoulder to find someone else to talk to?

Or, when selling, have you ever *known* that your potential customer is just not interested? In fact, they have totally switched off ...

Again, I bet you have. Everybody has.

But why is this? Why doesn't business communication work? Why can't people keep their audiences listening to them?

Because of one simple reason:

> **Business people say too much irrelevant stuff**
>
> - all the time
> - every day
> - to every type of person.

Think about it. It's true. Do any of these (totally irrelevant to you) things sound familiar?

- presentations that begin with the presenting company's year of formation, number of offices and staffing levels;
- networking conversations that include a lengthy description of the other person's company, their product range, infrastructure and history; or
- sales pitches that give a full, excruciatingly detailed description of how the product works (much of which you just don't need or even want to know).

Totally, utterly irrelevant to you. But you hear them all the time.

And, hand on heart, you probably do it too.

When you speak like this, it's very much like filling a bucket with jelly, and flinging it at the other person, hoping some of it will stick.

Some will, sure. But most won't. And it's *doubly* inefficient. It wastes your effort, money, resources and that priceless commodity ... time. And that of the people you talk to.

But there's an even bigger problem with 'jellying' someone. When you're on the receiving end, when it's *you* all this jelly is being flung at, you feel like you're on the receiving end of a big wet, useless barrage. A needless barrage. You feel like a target, not a person.

It puts you off doing what they want ... from buying into them and their ideas.

And flipping it round, when it's you 'jellying' someone else, they don't always do what you want either. Or buy into you. Or your ideas.

But imagine how much more you could achieve if you could overcome all this. Imagine if you knew how to say *only* the stuff that was 100% relevant to your audience.

Can you see how much more impact you would have?

Saying the right things in the right way – with no jelly – would help you get better results than ever before.

You'd be better at talking to others, at presenting, at networking, at selling. You would excel in interviews, meetings, pay-rise discussions ...

The benefits to you would be endless. You would have better business relationships, better personal relationships. Your business would grow much faster. You would make more money. You'd feel less frustrated by inefficient communication than you do now. Your communications would be quicker, more dynamic. You'd feel a real buzz of success, experience less of the dreaded feeling 'there's one that got away'. The list goes on and on ...

Because, when you think about it, to succeed you only need to answer 'yes' to two questions:

1   Are you good at your job?
2   Given that you are good at your job, do you get the results *some-body as good as you should get*?

Now I assume that, if you answered those two questions honestly, you'll have answered 'yes' and 'no'. If this is the case – and 100% of people I have asked these two questions do answer in this way – there's only really one skill you need to turn your answers into 'yes, yes' ...

For you to achieve the results someone with your abilities should get ...

... the only skill you need to master is ...

... the ability to *persuade others how good you are.*

You simply need to convince others of your skills, your ability to help them ... then watch your business grow.

And that's what you'll learn from this book. I'll show you how to master 'the only skill you need': how to communicate *persuasively*, so that your communications *work – every time*.

By the time you have finished this book, you will know how to say only *relevant* stuff to others, so that you never 'jelly' anyone again.

You'll learn what I have learned from speaking to my blind Mother, where it's essential that I communicate with her in such a way that she understands everything in *seconds*.

Because she doesn't have time for irrelevant jelly.

Nor do the people you talk to.

The AFTERs

3

HOW CAN YOU TELL IF COMMUNICATION HAS WORKED?

Would you consider these four outcomes to be successes?

- You attend a networking event, talk to lots of strangers, and come home with 26 people's business cards.
- You meet a potential customer over coffee at Starbucks. They're wowed by what you do, and praise your sales skills.
- One of your clients loves you to bits and says they'd recommend you to anyone.
- You make a presentation to 50 people. Although nervous beforehand, it goes well. They seem to like it, and laugh at all the right places ...

You've no doubt experienced similar scenarios. After all, networking, selling, seeking referrals and presenting are four of the most common 'communication situations' around.

So, if it was *you* who had 26 strangers' business cards, praise from a potential customer, an offer of referrals and a happy audience, would you think you'd done well? That your communications had *worked?*

At first glance, the four outcomes seem impressive. But, the only true barometer of whether communication is effective or not is what happens AFTER, and whether these AFTERs are enough for you.

So, 26 business cards is great, but does it grow your business? No. You've just turned strangers into non-strangers. Better AFTERs would be turning these non-strangers into contacts with whom you have a productive relationship.

Similarly, wowing a potential customer is a good start. But the only AFTER you want from a sales meeting … is a *sale*.

An existing customer offering to refer you? It's only good if – AFTER your chat with her – she actually *does* help you get sales meetings with her contacts.

And a presentation that seemed to go well? Well, presentations are only effective if they achieve what you wanted them to AFTERwards – winning the sale, the Board accepting your proposal, and so on.

So, communication is successful only if you get what you want AFTERwards, as Fig. 3.1 shows.

In other words, your ultimate AFTER with these four situations is the right-hand column: to *grow your business*.

And that's what this book does – help you grow your business by communicating in the best way, whether you're networking, selling, seeking referrals or making presentations.

THE AFTERS: THE SECRET INGREDIENT TO JELLY-FREE COMMUNICATION

When you look at Fig. 3.1, an important fact jumps out. As the author, column 2 is most interesting to me: after all, it's my expertise. I've

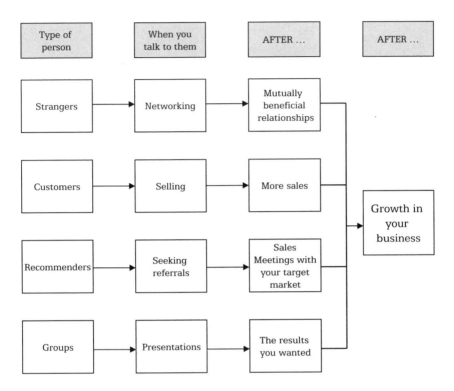

Figure 3.1 Successful communication.

structured this book around it: there's a main section for each of column 2's four areas.

But, to *you* – my audience – you're focussed on something *utterly different*. You're ultimately interested in column 4. You want this book to help you grow your business.

And this difference is an example of the principal reason why verbal communication often doesn't work well. *Because the speaker and their audience have different focuses.* Whereas the speaker focuses on their expertise, audiences don't care what you say – they only care what they are left with AFTER you've said it.

Audiences don't care what you say.

They only care what they are left with AFTER you've said it.

So delegates on an Excel course are interested in the time they'll save AFTER the course, not Excel itself.

You're focussed on the car you'll able to afford AFTER securing your car loan, not the loan.

But hardly anybody focuses on the audience's AFTERs when they speak. Excel trainers understandably think their delegates only want to learn Excel. They don't.

Car-loan arrangers think the loan's all-important. It's not.

When I tell people about the audience's AFTERs being so critical, they often reply, 'Why doesn't anyone focus on them then?' You might well be thinking the same. The best answer I have is simply that most people assume that traditional communication is the 'right way to do it'. *Because that's what everybody does.* But that doesn't make it *right*.

So, since audiences are only interested in their AFTERs, the sequence in which you present your ideas is critical to ensuring audiences engage, buy-in and, ultimately, act on what you say.

But, of course, it's not simply 'think of their AFTERs, and you will be fine' (though it's an excellent start, and is something you must do). There are five other rules which underpin the communication process, rules I've been developing all my life …

THE FIVE RULES OF COMMUNICATION

As you read in the preface, the rules governing how to communicate with blind people are totally transferable to business, because business people don't *see* things from your point of view.

This isn't just a hunch of mine. It's tested and proven. I *know* it's true because I've honed the techniques in this book for many years, in many different situations, with thousands of people, all over the world.

Now, given that speaking to business people and blind people is so similar, techniques that work with the latter will also work well with the former.

My mother and I have created the five rules of communicating with blind people. These have been refined and practised over the years. They are *right*.

And, now that you know they're totally transferable to sighted people, these are the five rules *you* must follow to have the maximum impact – and minimum jelly – when speaking to others:

1 always context first;
2 frame of the other person;
3 thoroughness is key;
4 'extra info?'; and
5 required info only.

Table 3.1 gives more detail on each rule, with an example of each from a blind person's point of view, and the reason why the rule is so important.

In many ways, these five rules are obvious. But, people often forget them when speaking. For instance, they don't put things in *context* for the other person first … often because they're not always quite sure what the context is. Or, they don't ask what extra information is needed, because they're not sure what information will come out of their mouth.

Let's see how to apply the rules to business using the example of making a sale. Imagine that you've prepared a beautiful PowerPoint presentation, and the first bullet point of slide 1 says: 'We were established in 1922.' Does your date of incorporation obey the five rules?

Rule	In other words	For example	Reason
Always context first	Explain the big picture first, so any subsequent detail is relate-able to something.	'You're sitting in a large rectangular room. Your chair is positioned at the side of the room, halfway along one of the short walls. To get to the door, stand up, turn right, walk three metres – there are no obstacles between you and the door.'	If you don't say the context first, the blind person won't know where she is *in relation to everything else*, meaning she might walk in the wrong direction/fall over furniture etc.
Frame of the other person	Think from the perspective *of the other person*: get into their skin.	'If I was you, and was at a Networking event, I'd need introducing to others since I couldn't see them to approach them. So, who would you like to speak to?'	Blind people face different challenges than we do and, to fully empathize with them, we have to place ourselves in their shoes.
Thoroughness is key	Expand on the relevant and important subjects, to give more detailed information.	'The floor is wooden, and has a big rectangular rug on it. The rug finishes one metre before you come to the door, so you will know when you're nearly there. It's a double door, with both doors opening towards you.'	You want the other person to feel comfortable and not embarrassed, so they easily (a) find the door, (b) are pre-warned of any unexpected obstacles, and (c) can open it when they get there.

'Extra info?'	Always ask if anything else would be helpful, so you know they have all the information they need.	'Does that tell you everything you need to know? Or is there anything else that would help you here?'	Don't *assume* the blind person has all the information they need, just because *you* think they have. Remember, to *assume* makes an '*ass*' of '*u*' and '*me*'
Required info only	Ask the other person what information they want, rather than flinging jelly at them, and hoping some sticks.	'Would you like me to tell you about colours, pictures on the wall, etc.?'	Some blind people might find it helpful to have this visual picture: it might, for instance, help them with subsequent conversation and to feel as integrated as possible with the room. However, other blind people are proud of their own world, and won't want information that's irrelevant to them. That's why it is essential to ask.

Table 3.1 The five rules you must follow to have the maximum impact – and minimum jelly – when speaking to others

Rule 1 – No, there is no *context* for the audience. They aren't sure why they should be listening to you yet. They can't see how your date of incorporation fits in with the overall picture. It is like saying to a blind person, 'There's a table 10 metres away.' The information might be relevant, but it's impossible for the blind person to tell, since she doesn't know where the table is *in relation to her journey*.

Rule 2 – No, it spectacularly fails the 'get into the skin' rule. Why should any customer even begin to care how old your company is? And, even if it did interest them a little, would they really want to hear about it *first*?

Rule 3 – No, this rule is about giving more detail on *relevant* and *important* subjects. Since your date of incorporation is neither, there is no need to expand on it.

Rule 4 – Not applicable. It's too early to tell, since you only ask if your audience wants any other information once you've told them everything you think they want to hear.

Rule 5 – No, you clearly haven't found out what is wanted, if the first thing you tell them is how old you are, rather than whether you are any good!

So, stating your date of incorporation first in a sales pitch fails four of the rules, and isn't applicable to the other.

In fact, stating your date of incorporation is rife throughout the business world, and I've never understood why. Your audience doesn't *care*. They just want to know if you can help them. If you were founded in 1922, does this make you better/worse than someone who was founded in 1921? Or 1962? Of course not. So, it's *irrelevant* and won't differentiate you. It's a great example of the jelly that people fling.

The best way to remember the five rules

This chapter contains two invaluable pieces of advice:

- AFTERs, and
- the five rules of communication.

By the end of this book, AFTERs will be second nature to you. But how to remember the five rules? There are so many things to remember these days, how can you remember five different rules? Well, have a look at the initials again:

Always context first

Frame of the other person

Thoroughness is key

Extra info?

Required info only

The simple way to learn and recall the five rules is by remembering their initials spell the one word that drives jelly-free communication: AFTER.

THE BEST TYPE OF ADVICE IS ANNOYINGLY SIMPLE

When Sir Alex Ferguson first became Manager at Manchester United Football Club, it was three years before he won his first trophy. That's a long time for a club like Manchester United, and the English press were smelling blood. There were countless newspaper 'exclusives' relaying in detail how he was about to be sacked.

Sir Alex discussed the adverse press coverage with former Manchester United Manager, Sir Matt Busby, saying how every time he opened a newspaper there seemed to be yet another unpleasant article about him. He told Sir Matt that reading all these articles was depressing him.

Sir Matt Busby's advice?

'Stop reading them then.'

A great tip. And pretty obvious, really. But why is it all the best advice is so *annoyingly simple*?

Just as Sir Alex Ferguson needed someone else to point out a simple way to solve something troubling him, so too did *I* need the intervention of someone else to solve something I'd been wrestling with for years.

During my time teaching accountants how to pass their professional exams, I was often asked, 'Why are you so good at explaining things?' To which my inspired answer was always, 'Dunno. Just am.'

A totally unsatisfactory response. It made me wonder why I could explain the complexities of accountancy so people could understand it in *seconds*, but I couldn't explain to anyone – including myself – why I was so good at explaining things in general.

And then – just like Sir Alex Ferguson – someone pointed out the answer which, in retrospect, was so *obvious*.

I was talking to my mother about Beth McDevitt, a student of mine who had recently become a national prize-winner in her accountancy exam. I was telling Mum how pleased I was for her – Beth had worked hard, and thoroughly deserved her success.

Mum replied: 'I know I'm biased because I'm your mother, but you probably had something to do with it too. I guess you're good at explaining things to people because you're so good at explaining things to me.'

And that was it. I suddenly got it. It was so *obvious* – like the advice not to read newspapers if newspapers are saying horrible things about you. It was only *then* I realised why I was good at explaining things: because of all those years explaining things to Mum.

AFTERs and the five rules underpin successful jelly-free communication, whether you're networking, selling, seeking referrals or making presentations.

They work:

- for every audience;
- in any setting; and
- on any day,

as you're about to discover …

Networking

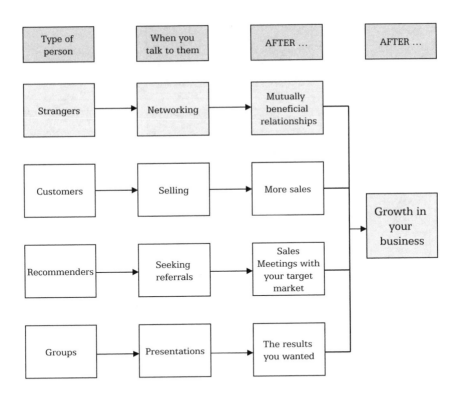

Type of person	When you talk to them	AFTER ...	AFTER ...
Strangers	Networking	Mutually beneficial relationships	
Customers	Selling	More sales	Growth in your business
Recommenders	Seeking referrals	Sales Meetings with your target market	
Groups	Presentations	The results you wanted	

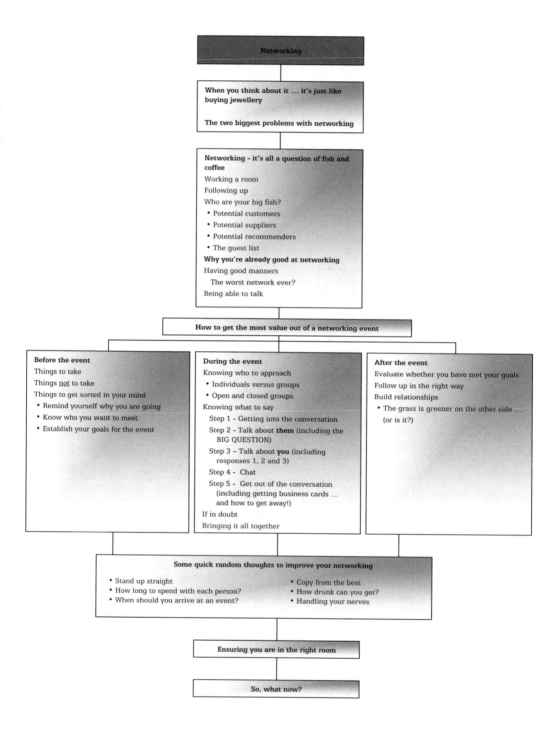

WHEN YOU THINK ABOUT IT ... IT'S JUST LIKE BUYING JEWELLERY

George and Mary are one of the nicest couples you could ever meet. They're both in their forties, and have been happily married for over twenty years – very much the classic 'childhood sweethearts'. George is a keen gardener; Mary sings in the local choir; they go to church together every Sunday.

Recently though, George has been getting worried. He's not good at buying romantic presents, and their silver wedding anniversary is next week.

George is the type of man who buys functional gifts. You know the type of thing ... a new atlas because the old one was out of date, a steam iron which he thinks will make Mary's life easier, a carrier bag holder for the kitchen.

But, with it being a special occasion, he wants to give Mary something she'll treasure forever. So George has decided to buy jewellery. The trouble is that he's never bought jewellery before. He doesn't even know where to go to buy it, nor does he know the type of thing Mary likes.

After a great deal of worrying, George sets off to a large store down-town that he's heard has a wide selection of products, at good prices.

But, when he gets there, he hates the sense of bustle, and that every-one else seems to know each other, and where they're going.

He looks round, but doesn't see any jewellery, so doesn't know which direction to walk. And, because everybody is speaking to somebody else, he doesn't know who to approach – after all, he doesn't want to break up a conversation just because he doesn't know where he's going.

So, George does the only thing he can think of – he wanders round aimlessly, hoping to find the jewellery section. But he can't find it *anywhere*. He starts feeling embarrassed because, although nobody else seems to be looking at him, he knows that they probably are. And that they probably think it's funny how out of place he looks.

Eventually, he wanders over to a sullen-looking teenager standing on her own, and asks her. But she's no help. He perseveres with her nevertheless – after all, she's the easiest person for him to speak to.

But, after ten wasted minutes, he realises this too is pointless. He says to himself, 'I've had enough. I'm going to ask the cashier.'

He walks over and says, 'I'm looking to buy my wife some jewellery for our silver wedding, but I just can't find it *anywhere*.'

The cashier replies: 'You've not been here before, have you sir?'

George's heart sinks. He knows he must look so out of place. All George can mumble is, 'Not as such, no,' to which the cashier replies:

'I didn't think so. This is a book store.'

THE TWO BIGGEST PROBLEMS WITH NETWORKING

Why tell you George's story?

Because it mirrors *exactly* the two biggest problems people find when networking:

1   People don't work the room well (just like George, who didn't approach anyone except the grumpy teenager); and …
2   … they're not even in the *right room* in the first place!

Networking's everywhere these days. You just can't avoid it. There are more events now than ever, always packed with people who could be very useful to you.

Because there are so many events, it is imperative that you:

- go to the right ones (it's no use going if there aren't any useful people); and
- when you're there, do the right things: speak to the *right* people, in the *right* way, for the *right* length of time … to get the *right* result.

This section will help you grow your business when networking.

To start, here's my definition of networking … I imagine it's not what you've heard before …

NETWORKING – IT'S ALL A QUESTION OF FISH AND COFFEE

The dictionary defines networking as 'interacting or engaging in informal communication with others for mutual assistance or support'.

My definition is somewhat different. I devised it when working with BNI's directors. (BNI is the world's largest networking and referral organisation, with 100,000 members in 30 countries.)

Now, if you're teaching the directors of the world's largest networking organisation how to teach networking, there's a fair bit of pressure because they're already experts at it. So, the first impression was vital.

Since the session was to start with a definition of networking, I thought I'd better give them something to think about. This is what I came up with …

Imagine a fishing boat hoisting its net out of the sea.

As it breaks through the water's surface, you see the net is full of three types of catch: big fish, tiddlers and some old boots that must have been thrown into the sea some time ago.

You'd expect to see seawater dripping from the bottom of the net back into the sea. Surprisingly, it's not seawater, but *coffee*. And, even more surprisingly, the coffee isn't dripping vertically; it's flowing *diagonally* downwards into a large coffee cup.

In short, a large net containing big fish, tiddlers and boots, from which coffee is pouring into a large coffee cup.

I guess you're surprised by this definition? The BNI directors certainly were! Let me explain what I mean …

There are two skills you need for networking to be effective:

- working a room; and
- following up.

Looking at each in turn:

Working a room

Imagine being in the middle of the net. You're surrounded on all sides by big fish (tasty, appetising), tiddlers (who'll provide some sustenance, but not much) and boots (which have no nutritional value at all).

It's the same when networking. You're in the middle of a room surrounded by people who are very useful to you ('big fish'), quite useful ('tiddlers') and no use ('boots'). You have to work your way round the room, meeting and impressing as many big fish as possible.

Following up

People don't tend to close many sales at networking events. I mean – have *you* ever sold anything when networking? When you think about it, the odds on meeting someone who (a) wants your product (b) at that precise point in time (c) to such an extent they don't want to speak to anybody else in the room is – at best – remote.

Since you are unlikely to get a sale there, the best you can hope for is to arrange a subsequent meeting over a cup of coffee, to get to know each other much better.

Therefore – and this is *the big point* – the ultimate aim of networking is **not** to work your way round the net. Instead, it's to arrange to have a cup of coffee with a big fish, *on a subsequent date*.

This realisation makes networking much easier. Because, once you see your only aim is to arrange a subsequent cup of coffee, (and not to close a sale), there's less pressure on the night. Your goals are *so much easier to achieve*.

This chapter will show you the skills you need to get cups of coffee with your big fish. You'll learn how to get in and out of conversations, which groups of people to approach, and which to leave alone. I'll show you how to introduce yourself so people think you're worth talking to, and the right questions to ask so they are pleased that they spoke to you.

The first step to address is …

Who are your Big Fish?

A big fish is your ideal type of person to meet when networking, and will be some/all of the following:

- potential customers;
- potential suppliers;

- potential recommenders; and
- the guest list.

Potential customers

One of the first things to know in business is what a potential customer looks like. If you don't, how can you tell when you bump into one?

In George Orwell's book *Animal Farm*, there's the famous quote: 'All animals are equal, but some animals are more equal than others.' And it's *exactly* the same with customers: 'All customers are equal, but some customers are more equal than others.'

Some customers give you more than others, in terms of income and/or your pleasure from working with them. *These* are your big fish – the people you want to meet when networking.

My personal trainer Greg and his wife Charlotte are both great friends of mine – between them, they've helped me reduce my bodyweight by a third (I used to be rather large!).

It's their pasts which make them so good at their jobs. Greg used to be a marine and a paramedic; Charlotte, a professional dancer and trained sports masseuse. (A word of warning – and this is the best advice in this book – *never* say to an ex-marine personal trainer, 'There's nothing you can do in this training session which will hurt me.' I said it only once – about six months ago – and I've only just recovered ...)

As a thank you to them for helping me lose all this weight, I said I'd help them get more clients. I started off by asking them what a customer looks like to them. They said '25–35, professional, live locally'.

I could see why they'd say this – after all, it described their typical customer. But I said, 'Isn't it someone who'll use you 2–3 sessions per week forever, and tell all their friends about you?'

They agreed. My simple sentence changed the focus of our chat, and subsequently the focus of their business, which has rocketed since they discovered what an ideal customer looked like, and focused on finding lots of them.

Which brings me back to *your* business. To find *your* ideal customers, look down your current customer list, and highlight the ones who:

- pay you the most money;
- you enjoy working with most; or
- you've had the most success with.

These are the ones who give you the biggest return. For instance, you might have identified:

- customers who have paid the most money:
  - a bank (the marketing department is your contact there);
  - an IT company (the sales team).
- customers who you most enjoy working with:
  - you worked with a national charity at a reduced cost, which – although didn't pay well for you – was the most satisfying work you did last year.
- who you had the most success with:
  - you spent one day consulting with a small local accountancy practice; following your advice, they won an enormous contract, which changed their business beyond recognition.

This makes your big fish – the people you're *itching* to meet at networking events:

- banks, especially someone in a marketing department;
- sales directors of IT companies;

- senior people in large charities; and
- an employee of your local accountancy institute.

The top three are self explanatory. But the fourth warrants a second look. Why 'local accountancy institute', and not 'other small accounting firms'?

Well, the small accountancy firm only spent one day with you, with no prospect of further work, so they're not a long-term profitable client for you, not a big fish.

But, if you could get access to lots of accounting firms in one go, via someone at the local accountancy institute, *that* would be a great contact. So, the institute is a big fish; whereas one small firm would be a tiddler.

Also, (and we'll look at this more in the 'Potential recommenders' section) *someone who knows someone* from the above list is also a big fish. For example, if the area manager of your bank knew the marketing director of her bank, she would go on the list too, since she has the power to recommend you in.

So your big fish are now:

- bank – senior marketing person, or someone who knows a senior marketing person;
- IT – sales director, or someone who knows a sales director;
- charity – senior decision maker, or someone who knows a senior decision maker; and
- local accountancy institute – senior decision maker, or someone who knows a senior decision maker.

And do you know the weirdest thing? Once you know *exactly* who you want to bump into, you're much more likely to bump into them! Here are three possible reasons – choose your favourite:

1   'You get what you expect in this life.' If you think a day is going to be dreadful, it probably will be; and vice versa. It's the same with people – if you expect to meet certain professions, you tend to.

2   'The harder I practise, the luckier I get' (Gary Player, golfer). The harder you practise finding big fish, the luckier you'll be in actually finding them. (Also talking of *luck*, Robert, my father-in-law and a mathematician, says there's no such thing. He thinks luck is simply a combination of *probability* and *hard work*; and *working hard* to find your big fish certainly increases the *probability* of it happening.)

3   Your *reticular activator* (described by Masters in the making as '… a net-like group of cells in [your] brain that acts as a natural filtering device, which allows those things [you] see as a benefit or a threat to become a part of [your] awareness'). You will have experienced this before. For instance, when you last bought a new car, you'll have seen about 17 other identical cars as you drove home from the garage! You're aware of these cars now because it matters to you. It's the same with big fish: once you know who *matters* to you, you'll see lots of them.

This works on all levels – let's try a little experiment now. Stop reading this book at the bottom of this paragraph and look round the room for ten seconds. Count how many *blue* things you can see. OK, do it now …

Have you done it? How did you do?

Now, without looking round the room, think how many *brown* (not *blue)* things there are.

I guess less brown than blue? But, if you look round the room for *brown* now, you'll see there's more than you thought. The brain sees things that it's focusing on. So, you focusing on banks, IT companies, charities and accountancy institutes means you are more likely to find them when networking.

Potential suppliers

Depending on your job, good suppliers could be at least as important to you as good customers. This could be suppliers for your business, or for your *clients'* businesses. Let me explain …

When my business started, I needed all the normal 'business start-up stuff' – a website, a brand, IT, staff, stationery, finances etc. So, when networking, I knew that if I met good suppliers in these fields, they might be able to help me.

My reticular activator was fully switched on. One person I met was Ian Denny, the managing director of an IT company. I got on really well with him, realised his company could help me, and they did a great job for me.

Suppliers for your business are big fish. But so, too, are potential suppliers for your *clients*.

Imagine one of your key clients saying how embarrassed they feel because of the shoddy look of their brochures. You tell them you know a good graphic designer who could revamp their brochures. You put the two of them together. The graphic designer does a fantastic piece of work, which delights your client …

How good does that make you feel? How good does that make you *look*?

That's great customer service. You didn't benefit financially from the transaction at all – after all, your client paid the graphic designer, not you – but think of all the other benefits to you: enhanced relationship with both your client and the designer, greater loyalty from your client, increased likelihood of more business. These are all *such hard goals* to achieve, but you've achieved them just by recommending a graphic designer you already knew.

It is my firm belief that clients seek out suppliers who can solve their problems, and they have *lots* of problems they want solving, and not just in your area. The more problems you help them solve, the more you stand out as a *great* supplier!

A word of warning here. Your relationship with your clients is everything. Just as you can improve your relationship by introducing a good graphic designer to them, recommend a bad one and your relationship may never recover. You must be *100% sure* that whoever you recommend will do a great job. If you *do* have any doubts, phrase your recommendation in such a way you are really honest with your client, maybe … 'I met a graphic designer at a recent networking event. I don't know his/her work, but I know that you are looking for one. It might be worth giving him/her a call.'

Getting back to our big fish list, let's say you could really do with a good financial advisor. Your finances are in a bit of a mess. Also, you know that one of your clients wants some brochures printed. Let's add these to your list, which now reads:

- bank – senior marketing person, or someone who knows a senior marketing person;
- IT – sales director, or someone who knows a sales director;
- charity – senior decision maker, or someone who knows a senior decision maker;
- local accountancy institute – senior decision maker, or someone who knows a senior decision maker;
- financial advisor (for me) – or someone who knows a good financial advisor; and
- graphic designer (for my client) – or someone who knows a good graphic designer.

This list contains some useful people. But there is an even more valuable person you can meet when networking …

Potential Recommenders

Someone who recommends you to other people is potentially the most valuable business contact you can have, because of the amount of business they can bring you. Imagine a business contact who recommends you to one new client per month. How valuable would they be? Certainly more so than any single client – they only give you one piece of business ... their own! But someone who gives you business month after month after month ... they are *gold dust*.

Section 6 is devoted to how to trigger recommendations from your business contacts, but – for now – let's keep it very simple.

Ask yourself: 'Who would know lots of people on my big fish list?'

For instance, a good lawyer will know lots of bankers. So, even though a lawyer isn't a potential client, they know people who are.

Adding potential recommenders to your big fish list:

- bank – senior marketing person, or someone who knows a marketing person;
- IT – sales director, or someone who knows a sales director;
- charity – senior decision maker, or someone who knows a senior decision maker;
- local accountancy institute – senior decision maker, or someone who knows a senior decision maker;
- financial advisor for me – or someone who knows a good financial advisor;
- graphic designer for my client – or someone who knows a good graphic designer;
- lawyers (recommend you to banks);
- telephone systems installers (recommend you to IT companies);
- CSR senior personnel (recommend you to charities);

- heads of other professional bodies (recommend you to the accountancy institute);
- will-writers (recommend you to financial advisors); and
- marketing companies (recommend you to graphic designers).

There are now twelve professions on this list. What are the chances of meeting at least one of them when networking? Pretty good, I'd say. In fact, I'd be surprised if you didn't.

Imagine two identical businessmen networking. One has the above list in her head; the other doesn't. Who would do better? The answer is obvious. You need your reticular activator on.

A quick thought

Before reading on, why not create your big fish list now?

The guest list
Some networking events allow you to see the guest list beforehand. Get hold of one if you can to see which big fish are on there.

Not only does this give you an idea of who to look for on the night, but you might also see a big fish on the list who you hadn't thought of previously.

I always used to marvel at how well my father did this. He used to be Chief Executive of Liverpool City Council, and therefore got invited to hundreds of events, dinners and the like. He'd always study the guest list intently before the night, and without exception ended up talking to the people he wanted to.

Networking is hard enough. Don't make it harder by not knowing who you want to speak to.

Why you're already good at networking

People often think networking is tricky. And, to be fair, some of it does take time to master.

However – and this might surprise you – you are already very good at two of the core skills you must possess to succeed …

Add these two existing strengths to the fact that you're only seeking to have a 'cup of coffee with a big fish at a later date', and networking is becoming much less onerous than it first appeared.

The two skills that I know you possess, even though I don't actually know *you,* are:

- having good manners; and
- being able to talk.

Let's look at why these are so critical to success.

Having good manners

Display good manners when networking, and you're well on the way to being brilliant at it. Well-mannered people:

- ask about other people before talking about themselves;
- don't butt into conversations;
- don't look over your shoulder when you're speaking, because they're looking for someone more interesting to speak to;
- show interest in what you say;
- won't aggressively sell to you on a first meeting;
- won't walk off having spoken about themselves, without asking about you; but will
- wait to be asked, before talking in depth about themselves.

Have you ever been on the receiving end of any of these? My most memorable experience of this happened in 2004. I can still remember it as if it was yesterday …

The worst networking ever?

At the time, I weighed about 280 pounds (127 kg). I don't now – far from it – but I did.

I was hosting a chamber of commerce event in Liverpool. As host, I could speak about my business, to market it to everyone there.

I decided not to just rant on about myself, but instead to advise the attendees how to get most business from the night.

One thing I covered was that they shouldn't sell to the room, but – instead – should seek to build relationships.

After my talk, a gentleman approached me, a huge smile on his face, and thanked me, saying, 'Normally, when I come to these things, I dread the bit where the host stands up and sells their business. But you didn't do that. You gave some great advice. Thank you.'

And, we started chatting. And then he said …

'Yes, I really enjoyed everything you said. But if you don't mind me saying … you're very *fat*.'

Well I *was* surprised. And, as many people do when surprised, said 'I beg your pardon?'

And he said it *again*. Word for word. And once again, with emphasis on the word *fat*.

This time, I didn't answer. I didn't know what to say.

And so he carried on … 'And because you're *fat*, you're putting extra weight on your lower back. Well I sell lumbar supports …'

True story. This man, having attended the event I'd paid for, eaten the food I'd provided, heard me say not to sell to the room … had come over, and told me that, because I was fat, I needed to buy his product.

Needless to say, this gentleman didn't get the sale he was after and – joking apart – nor will anybody else if they are ill-mannered when networking. Good manners underpin every aspect of networking and, since you have them already, you're well on the way to having the basics you need to excel.

Being able to talk

You've been practising talking all your life. If you think of conversations as having a beginning, middle and an end, you're very good at all three when talking to others.

There are certain lines you must say at the *beginning* and *end* of networking conversations (this chapter will teach you both), but the *bulk* of the conversation (the middle bit); you can already do, because it's just talking.

> You already possess two of the core skills needed to be good at networking – good manners and the ability to chat. You just need to know how to use these existing skills in a new context.

HOW TO GET THE MOST VALUE OUT OF A NETWORKING EVENT

I can't drive, but my understanding of driving is that all the individual actions involved – from turning the steering wheel to changing gear – are quite easy to master on their own. But, when you're learning, putting everything together is the hard bit.

After a time, though, you get used to doing everything at the same time, and it becomes second nature.

Networking is identical to driving in this respect. All the individual actions are quite straightforward on their own, but it takes practice for everything to work well together.

To get maximum value from any event you attend, you need to master what to do:

1   before the event;
2   during the event; and
3   after the event.

Many people think the second one – what you do *during* the event – is the most important. In fact, that's wrong. All three are equally important.

In fact, there's even an argument that what you do *during* the event is the *least* important … because, if you don't get your preparation right beforehand (for instance, if you didn't know your big fish) and you don't follow-up properly afterwards, networking just isn't going to work for you anyway.

Before the event

Things to take

Let's do the easy stuff first. These are the two essentials you must take:

- your business cards; and
- a pen.

Without the former, you can't give your contact details/something to remember you by; without the latter, you can't write. As you'll see throughout this chapter, you'll be doing lots of writing as you work the room.

It's also worth your taking a third item: a name badge. People approach you more if you wear one. These could be strangers (who know they can start a conversation with, 'Hello Andy'); or they could be people you've met before, who can't remember your name, so wouldn't have approached you through embarrassment.

These are the main name badge rules:

- It's your first name people want to know, so make it easy to read.
- If you want to add your surname, do so, but it is not essential.
- Therefore, simply attaching your business card to your lapel is not enough (your name won't be large enough to read). You need to specifically create a name badge.
- Include a few words underneath your name so others can identify if you're one of their big fish. This could be the name of your company, or – more likely – your profession.
- Wear your name badge as high up as possible, so people can read it easily. Wearing it on a long strap so people have to gaze at your navel isn't that helpful. I once saw someone with their name badge clipped to their belt buckle – now that's just *not* going to work.
- Wear your name badge on the right hand side. People shake hands using their right hand, so, your right hand side naturally moves towards them.

Always take your business cards, a pen, and a name badge.

Things not to take

I was once running a networking workshop for a bank, and asked them, 'What should you *not* take to a networking event?'

Their answers made it very clear my question had not been specific enough. Some of the more memorable responses included: a horse, a sword, seven bags of sugar and a tent.

You know that feeling of 'hmm, I didn't really give clear enough direction there, did I?'

The point I was making – and am doing now – is that your company marketing material is *not* needed when you network, so don't take it. This might seem strange to you, but:

- Your only goal is to arrange a cup of coffee with a big fish at a later date. You don't need your marketing material to do this.
- You are not there to sell to the room; you are working around the net to find as many big fish as possible.
- The cornerstone of good networking is having good manners. People won't want to sit through a run-through of your marketing material.

Some reasons people propose for taking marketing material, and my responses to each, are shown in Table 4.1.

Reason for taking	My responses …
'To sell my product'	• You're networking, not selling; and • You'll make more sales over your subsequent cup of coffee than you ever could on the night. Take your marketing material then.
'To explain what I do'	This section includes a section on how to explain what you do in a way that is more engaging then any brochure could ever be.
'People might want to see it – won't I look daft if I haven't got it with me?'	I can't think of a better excuse for organising a cup of coffee!
'I'll miss out on any impulse purchases that people might make'	Yes, you might, but: • Impulse purchases at networking events are very rare; and • If any paperwork is involved, you are going to have to meet them at a later date anyway.
'My competitors always bring their brochures with them'	• All the reasons outlined here show that taking brochures is unwise; and • So, your competitors are doing something unwise, which is good for you. Your aim is to outdo, not copy them. Especially when they do unwise things.
'I absolutely need this document to explain succinctly what I do. It can't be done without it'	You can always simplify things using the tips I'll show you later in this section.

Table 4.1 My overall thought: brochures are full of irrelevant jelly – don't take them

Things to get sorted in your mind

Taking business cards, your best fountain pen and a name badge is a great start, but there's still plenty to do before you turn up at the event.

Very few people do everything I'm about to share with you. Do them all, every time, and you'll be ahead of the game.

Remind yourself why you are going

Remember the aim of networking: coffee with a big fish.

So, a networking event is simply a means to an end, nothing more. Don't think of it as anything more important than this.

Know <u>who</u> you want to meet

You know this from the big fish section (page 27). Don't forget, prepare your list *before* the event including (if it's appropriate) asking your host for the guest list.

Establish your goals for the event

A website designer I know in Liverpool goes to lots of networking events … I mean, pretty much all of them. He's one of these people about whom you think, 'Is there *only one* of him? He's in every single room I go in. He must be cloned.'

I don't know him particularly well, but we had a chat recently during which he told me that all his networking rarely works for him.

'What do you mean? What doesn't *work* about it?' I asked. To which he replied: 'Well, nothing ever comes of it.'

So, I pressed further: 'What do you want to come of it?'

His response: 'I don't know. More business, I suppose.'

I guess you can see the problem he had. Unless you know *exactly* what you want to get out of a networking event, you are not very likely to achieve it.

You know you want cups of coffee with big fish, but that needs breaking down more. Although a good golden rule, it's too vague.

No doubt, you've heard how goals should be SMART – Specific, Measurable, Achievable, Relevant, Timescaled. 'A cup of coffee with a big fish' isn't specific enough.

So what goals could you have?

Goal 1: 'I'm going to meet three big fish tonight.'
A great goal – it's S, M, A, R and T. Achieve it, have that cup of coffee with all three big fish, and the event's been a huge success.

But there's one problem.

It's *not controllable* by you. What if there aren't three big fish in the room? That means you've failed to meet your goal, through no fault of your own.

So, the goal might not be A-achievable. Also, it *can't* be a good goal if you don't have control over your achievement of it. Let's try something else.

Goal 2: 'I'm going to meet as many big fish as possible.'
This certainly gets rid of the uncontrollability of goal 1, but this one's hard to M-measure. How do you know if you've done well?

Also, you might stop too early, thinking 'I've met two big fish, that's a success', when there were actually another eighteen in the room.

No, we're going to need something else.

Goal 3: 'I'm going to speak to Mr X and Mrs Y from the guest list – if they actually turn up!'
A goal that's S, M, A, R *and* T.

However, you could go further. Professor Z might be in the room (an even bigger fish than either Mr X or Mrs Y). So, although a good goal, relying solely on the guest list is too restricting. It could mean that you miss some great opportunities.

How are we doing so far?

Goals 1 and 2 are insufficient. Goal 3 is much better, but it's not enough on its own. If anything, it should be an add-on to a main goal, which we have yet to find …

Goal 4: 'I'm going to speak to five strangers, and establish if they are a big fish or not. If they are, I'm going to arrange a cup of coffee with them.'
This is much better. It's SMART. And, focussing on *strangers* (and not big fish) is the key here. You *can't* control whether someone is a big fish (goal 1's problem), but you *can* control if you speak to a stranger or not.

Also, this goal has two supporting goals that make it work:

1   establish if they are a big fish; and
2   organise a cup of coffee if they are.

This type of goal-setting is called 'activity-based'. This means you are basing your goals solely on the *activities* you are going to do – *talking* to strangers, *establishing* if they're a big fish, *organising* cups of coffee.

Traditional goal-setting is 'result-based', where you are striving to achieve a particular *outcome*. For instance, goal 1 ('I'm going to get the *result* of three big fish') was like this.

The best thing about activity-based goal-setting is that you are always *in control* of whether you achieve it or not.

The best goal to have?

Whenever I network, my goal is a combination of goals 4 and 3. I set out to speak to five strangers (and do the right thing if they turn out to be big fish), then often add to that by saying ,'And I also want to make sure that I speak to Mr X on the guest list.'

This gives me utter clarity in what I'm looking to achieve from an event, and total control over whether I do so.

During the event
So, now to the event. You've prepared everything you need to take:

- big fish list;
- goals for the night;
- business cards;
- pen; and
- name badge, positioned correctly.

Also, don't forget you already possess the two skills that underpin your success when networking:

- having good manners; and
- being able to talk.

So, how to work the room? What must you do to meet as many big fish as possible?

There are only two further skills to have:

- knowing who to approach; and
- knowing what to say.

You will maximise your opportunities if you master both. Taking each in turn …

Knowing who to approach

Do you remember when you used to sit exams at school? There was always that dreaded moment when, every time you were struggling, you looked up and saw that *every single person in the room* was writing. Mostly, they were smiling, looking like they were finding the exam easy ... and you knew that – for some reason – the exam was worse for you than for them.

Networking is exactly the same. Every time you feel nervous, you can guarantee that – when you look up – *every single person in the room* is fully engrossed in a riveting chat. They are smiling. They look like they are finding networking easy. And you know – without any shadow of doubt – that networking is worse for you than it is for them.

Now, if everybody thinks it's 'worse for me than it is for them', the only logical conclusion is that it's very nerve-racking for *everybody*. Very few people enter a room of strangers and think, 'Fantastic – what a marvellous opportunity. A whole room of people who don't know me. I can't wait to meet them all, impress them and change their lives.'

I once heard a quote by a fantastic professional speaker called Marie Moseley, who said: 'Never compare your *inside* to somebody else's *outside*. Because you'll always lose.'

To me, that sums up how many people feel when networking. You feel nervous *inside*, but everybody else looks OK on the *outside*. But, you can't see their *inside* – and, believe me, they will be as nervous as you.

I have found that by far the most effective way to reduce your initial nerves is knowing *who* to approach. Unless you know this when you first enter the room, there's always that blind panic of 'where do I start?', and you often end up lurching towards the person you know best.

Fortunately, there are some simple guidelines which make it easy to know which groups to approach when you enter a room.

Before I run through them, take a good look at figure 4.1. Who would you speak to first?

Figure 4.1 People in a room.

There are 20 people in the room, so there are 20 people you could approach. Or so it seems ...

In fact, that's wrong. There are only a *very few people* you can approach here. And, knowing who to approach first greatly reduces your initial nerves.

Individuals versus groups

The first step is to split the room into individuals and groups.

There were two individuals in the room. In many ways, individuals are easier to approach than groups, because:

- speaking to one person is less daunting than to many;
- since they are on their own, they are probably glad of conversation, so they're likely to welcome you; and
- because they are on their own, you are not interrupting a group discussion.

So, in this room, you have at least two clear places you could start.

Open and closed groups

But, what if there weren't any individuals when you entered the room, only groups? Or, there was someone on their own, but you didn't want to approach him or her for some reason (for instance, because you didn't particularly like them).

Look at couple A (Fig. 4.2a) and couple B (Fig. 4.2b) below. Which could you approach? Either? Neither? Both?

Figure 4.2a Couple A – 'open two'.

Figure 4.2b Couple B – 'closed two'.

There is only one correct answer here: couple A, not couple B. You can tell from their body language. Couple A are standing in what's known as an 'open two'. It's how many people stand when networking. Their body language is perfectly cordial, but shows that both parties are happy for others to join them, which you could do like this:

Figure 4.3 Joining an 'open two'.

Entering this open two means you have formed a new group of three. Obviously, you need to say the right words as you approach the group – you can't just barge in – and the next section will show you what to say.

But what about couple B who you can't approach? Their body language shows they're having a conversation that neither wants interrupting. They're both giving the other their full attention. You can tell because they are facing each other – their shoulders are parallel. This is a 'closed two', and neither person will want you to approach.

Open and closed groups don't have to be just two people. You can have open/closed groups of any size …

Figure 4.4a 'Open three'.

Figure 4.4b 'Closed three'.

Figure 4.4c 'Open four'.

Figure 4.4d 'Closed four'.

Simple rule

Approach individuals and open groups only.

So, let's go back to the room plan you saw on page 48. Although there are 20 people in the room, you now know there are only 5 places you can go …

Figure 4.5 People you can approach.

Can you see how this knowledge makes a huge difference? It totally eliminates the dreaded feeling of 'everyone is in a conversation and I don't know where to start.'

> **'Yeah, but ...'**
>
> As you're reading this, you'll no doubt have nagging voices in your head saying, 'Yeah, but ... what if X happens?' Here's the first ...
>
> **'Yeah, but ...** what if there are no open groups?'
>
> *Answer:* There will be. Closed groups are rare, because net-workers generally want to talk to as many people as possible, not have only a few, intimate conversations.
>
> If, however, this does happen to you, you've been unlucky. Simply go to the bar, get a drink and turn back to face the room. By the time you've done this, some of the groups will have become open, believe me.

Knowing what to say

A networking conversation must include five steps:

1   getting into the conversation;
2   talk about *them*;
3   talk about *you*;
4   chat; and
5   get out of the conversation.

Steps 2, 3 and 4 can happen in any order (though the above is best), but *all five must happen* every time.

Step 1 – Getting into the conversation

I spent a long time working out the best way to approach strangers. What could I possibly say to get a conversation going every time? Then it suddenly dawned on me that simplicity would probably work best. So, I devised the following sentence, which has worked every time:

'Hello, I'm Andy'

Inspired. It works because the only reply you get is, 'Hello, I'm [their name]' – and the conversation has started.

That's step 1 over!

However, 'Hello, I'm Andy' only works well with individuals, not groups. Imagine approaching an open two who are enjoying a pleasant chat. Then you barge in, proudly announcing that you're called Andy. Not good.

The rule when approaching groups of any size is to always *ask permission*. Something like:

- 'Do you mind if I listen in?'
- 'Do you mind if I join you?'
- 'Are you OK if I hang with you guys for a bit?'
- I don't really know anybody else here. Do you mind if I listen in?'

Anything like this will do. Choose one that works for you, and stick with it. The one I tend to use is the top one – 'Do you mind if I listen in?' I have found that people's response is always, 'Sure – no problem.'

And that's step 1 … you've started the conversation.

Simple summary of step 1

- Approaching **individuals**: 'Hello, I'm Andy', or ask permission.
- Approaching **open groups**: ask permission.

Step 2 – Talk about them

It's important you speak about the other person *first*. I always feel I've failed if strangers ask me questions about myself before I've found out things about them.

There are many reasons why it's important to do this:

- It's better manners to talk about the other person first (and networking is all about good manners, as you know).
- It shows interest in the other person and, logically, they're more likely to then show more interest in you.
- You can find out early on if they're a big fish, tiddler or boot, which will help determine the style and length of conversation.
- Most importantly, networking is all about helping other people, not trampling all over them. You've a much better chance of helping the person you're speaking to if you ask about them first. In fact, with any networking conversation, always think, 'How can I *help* this person?', not, 'Is this person *any use* to me?' As well as being the right way to behave, research shows helping others is the most likely way to generate new business for yourself. Speaking about their business first is a good start to achieving this.

The best way to get them speaking about themselves first is by *asking questions*.

Here are some useful networking questions (note they all begin with the typical 'question words' – why, who, what, etc.):

- *Who* do you work for?
- *What* do you do?
- *What* do you enjoy most about your business?
- *What's* your role within the business?
- *What* are the main changes that have occurred in your profession recently?
- *What* changes do you expect to happen in the foreseeable future?
- *When* did you get into this business?
- *Where* are you planning to take the business in the future?
- *Where* are you based?
- *Why* is your business so successful?
- *How* long have you been doing it?

- *How* did you get into this business?
- *How's* business?
- *How* many staff have you got?
- *How* many branches have you got?

The important thing with questions is *to be interested in* their answers. Don't be in a rush to ask the next question. You're trying to get a conversation going here, not trying to ask every question you can possibly think of. I mean, you can imagine how inappropriate this would be:

You: How's business?

Them: Well, to be honest, not so good. Things were going well but then we hit a real downturn. Things are bad. We could go bust any minute.

You: OK, and how did you get into the business in the first place?

An extreme example perhaps, but you really have to follow the answers they give. The line I find works best is, *'That sounds interesting. Tell me more about that.'* This shows my interest, and helps them go into more depth, which in turn helps me to get to know them much better, more quickly.

I would much rather they answered three questions in depth, rather than ten questions at a very shallow level.

Yeah, but ...

Question: Won't they feel like they're being interrogated?

Answer: No. This is what conversationalists do. If somebody asks with a genuine interest about me, my family, my business, my life ... how could I ever take offence at that?

The BIG QUESTION to ask

There's one other question I always ask during step 2:

> *'What professions are good contacts for you?'*

This is *by far* the most valuable networking question I know, because:

- it shows real interest in them;
- it helps me *help* them, since their answer means I can point them in the right direction; and
- as you'll see in step 5 later, their answer helps me extricate myself from the conversation with the maximum amount of integrity, politeness and respect.

Another reason it works so well is that it's a question people have rarely been asked before. So, it's stands out in their mind as being both (1) new and (2) beneficial to them. (Incidentally, these two points – newness and benefits – tie in to research by John Caples in the early 1920s as to the components of powerful advertising headlines. Caples found that newness and benefits-to-the-reader were the two most attention-grabbing attributes a headline could have. So my *BIG QUESTION* is, if you like, the networking equivalent of that.)

Simple summary of step 2

- Talk about them first.
- Ask lots of questions.
- Show interest in their replies.
- Ask the *BIG QUESTION*: 'What professions are good contacts for you?'

Step 3 – Talk about **you**

Your conversation is going very well so far. The whole process looks like this:

> *You: 'Hello, I'm Andy.'*
>
> *Them: 'Hello, I'm Bob.'*
>
> *You: 'What do you do, Bob?'*
>
> *Them: [Answers question, and your conversation is under way].*

A few minutes later, they will ask about *you*. Your answer *has* to be impressive.

Do you find most people's response to 'What do you do?' really boring? People say things like:

- I'm a banker;
- I'm an accountant;
- I'm a lawyer; or
- I'm a financial adviser.

Totally uninspiring.

The problem is these sentences describe what the person *is*, not what the person *does*. But I don't care what the person *is*. I didn't even ask that – I asked 'What do you *do*?' So, an answer like 'I *am* an accountant' is not only boring and uninspiring, but doesn't even address the question asked.

And, when you think about it, giving a boring response to the first question is very dangerous. Everyone knows the importance of first impressions. When networking, your answer to 'what do you do?' is the first impression you give of yourself.

When answering the 'what do you do?' question, there are only two things to remember:

- you don't want to give too much information (or they'll think 'I wish I hadn't asked – he's *still* talking'); and
- the information you give must be so *interesting* that they think, 'Tell me more about that.'

Here's a three step process to develop your response:

1 say one sentence, based on the AFTERs;
2 explain the need for your services, then mention the AFTERs again; and
3 it's now time to show off … but with no jelly!

Taking each in turn …

Response 1 – use one sentence, based on the AFTERs
When networking, people don't really care what your profession is. They're more interested in what you help your customers achieve. What legacies you leave behind *after* working with them.

So, in my case, people are more interested in the results I get for my clients, rather than the fact that I work on their communication.

So, when someone asks what I do, I say: 'I help companies get better results when they speak.'

This will always be followed with, 'What do you mean?' or, 'Tell me more about that,' which is exactly what I want. They want to know what I mean by the word *results*. They want to know what *legacies* I leave my clients with. This sentence of mine *invites more questions.*

It's certainly a more powerful response than 'I am a comunications consultant', for all sorts of reasons, not least because people have their own preconceptions about what a communications consultant does.

Table 4.2 gives good and bad responses four different professions could give as their first sentence. Note how the right-hand side is the AFTERs, i.e. what clients are left with AFTER benefiting from each profession.

Traditional (bad)	AFTERs-based (good)
I am an accountant.	I help people pay less tax.
I work in real estate.	I help people buy the property of their dreams.
I'm a business coach.	I help business owners sell their company for the maximum possible amount.
I'm a personal trainer	I make my clients more attractive to their ideal partner.

Table 4.2 Traditional versus AFTER-based responses

And the list goes on (in fact, there's a more extensive one on page 95 in the *How to sell more* section). You can see how the sentences on the right-hand side follow a similar format, each having three components:

1 'I'
2 a verb ('help', etc)
3 AFTERs your clients are left with.

And did you notice the final one ('I make my clients more attractive to their ideal partner')? A bit of humour never goes amiss with these things. Some good ones I've heard recently are:

- a computer trainer – 'I take the *pain* out of Windows';
- a nutritionist – 'I help people who are sick and tired of feeling sick and tired';
- an optician – 'People come and see me before they can't see me'; and
- a funeral arranger – 'People are dying to see me.'

So, why not devise your response 1 sentence now? Use the ideas in this section to help you – 'I', verb, AFTERs. Remember your *only aim* from this sentence is that people are interested enough to ask you more – you are not giving the full picture here.

Yeah, but …

Question: Don't I need to be more informative with my first sentence?

Answer: Not at all. You are hopefully going to be talking to this person about yourself for at least 2–3minutes. Your only aim with response 1 is that they want to hear response 2. Nothing else matters.

Response 2 – Explain the need for your services – then mention the AFTERs again

Once the other person has said, 'Tell me more' following your response 1 – which they will – your next sentence needs to draw them further into how important you are to business people. They already know your AFTERs (from response 1), but it now needs to become more *real* for them.

The best way to do this is via a two-part response. The aim of the first part is to tell them there is a need for what you do; the second is to reinforce the AFTERs you've just mentioned.

Let me explain. If my response 1 is: 'I help companies get results when they speak', it will be followed by: 'What do you mean? Tell me more,' to which I reply:

Part 1 (explaining the need)
'Well, you know when people communicate; they always want them to achieve something? It might be a sale following a sales pitch, or their staff buying into the company's new vision …'

Part 2 (AFTERs again)
'Well, I ensure that companies actually *do* get the results they want from their communications.'

Can you imagine having this conversation with me at a networking event? If so, you could probably envisage yourself agreeing with the first part of my answer, because you know there's a need for what I do.

And the fact that you're agreeing with the first part, means that I'm immediately becoming a useful person to, if not *you*, then certainly *somebody*.

Assuming you've bought into what I'm talking about, you are now going to ask more questions. Like, 'How do you do that?'

In fact, you're *bound* to ask those questions because I *haven't told you anything about what I do* really. I've only told you what I leave my clients with AFTER I've worked with them, and the fact that there are people out there who need my help.

Again, why not prepare your response 2 now using the above example as a guide ...

Response 3 – It's now time to show off ... but with no jelly!
When they follow up your response 2 with 'Tell me more', it's time to spend 30–60 seconds explaining what you do.

Again, you've got to be impressive here. Although they're interested in you, they won't be for long if you drone on and on, flinging every type of jelly imaginable. Here are four tips that will help you be jelly-free:

- Facts tell; stories sell. Mention something you did with a client recently. Stories are much more memorable than facts about your business.
- Use the words 'for instance' before any example you give. 'Well, I've written a lot of sales pitches. For instance, there was client X who ...'
- Differentiate yourself from your competitors by saying phrases like 'unlike others in my profession ...', or 'rarely in my industry ...', or 'unlike anyone else I've come across ...'
- Remember – it's always better to say too little than too much. They can always ask for more information if they want it.

Creating a good 30–60 seconds isn't easy, and takes time and effort. Unless you spend time practising, writing, editing, and asking other people's views, you will not sound as impressive as you actually are ... and that's a huge opportunity missed.

Again, why not look at this now? Remember to use the four tips above, and to *keep it brief.*

To make it even easier, why not ask your friends what they think your best things are. This would help you generate a really good list, from which you can choose your best.

A couple of templates for your 30–60 seconds to get you started:

- I ... [help ... AFTERs];
- I work with ... [your typical clients] ...
- to help them ... [your AFTERs in detail]
- like I did with ... [a client – by name, or just say 'one client'] ...
- who ... [tell the story] ...
- which meant they ... [list the benefits to them of what you did].

Or, how about:

> - I ... [help ... AFTERs];
> - and I work with ... [your typical clients] ...
> - who have a problem with...[the areas you sort for clients];
> - For instance ... [tell a story];
> - I was able to get this result because, unlike others in my profession, ... [differentiate yourself].

Simple summary of step 3

- Not 'I'm an accountant.'
- Response 1 – use one sentence, based on the AFTERs.
- Response 2 – explain the need for your services – then mention the AFTERs again.
- Response 3 – it's now time to show off – but with no jelly!
- Continually edit and re-edit until it's brilliant.
- Practise like mad.

Step 4 – Chat

The formal part of your conversation is over now. You got into the conversation with a stranger (step 1), and discovered interesting things about them (step 2), and have now explained what you do in the most interesting way possible (step 3).

The fifth and final step is what to do at the end of the conversation ... so what could step 4 possibly be? In many ways, steps 1, 2, 3 and 5 seem to cover everything.

Well, so far, the networking conversation has been very work-centric. You may well have found common ground during steps 2 and 3, but you probably haven't spent much time getting to know the other person on a more personal level.

Remember, your only target is a subsequent cup of coffee with a big fish, so you're not going to have a long chat here. However, a few friendly words will pay dividends in the future.

I know you won't need any guidance from me, – or anyone – on how to chat. But here are a couple of tips that might make step 4 work better for you:

- Before entering the room, arm yourself with 2–3 conversation topics you can drop in at any time. For instance, something on the news that day, a comment about the venue, the latest sports news, asking if the other person has attended similar events before, etc. This reduces any concerns you might have that you won't be able to think of anything to say.
- As a young man, I remember one piece of advice my Mother taught me when speaking to others: 'Find out what the other person is interested in. And talk about that.' This helps the conversation flow much more easily.
- Remember your manners when chatting. It's still crucial you don't go for the sale here, and remember to think 'How can I help this person?', not 'Is this person any use to me?'
- Be interested (in them), not interesting (about yourself).

And that's all the guidance you need for step 4. Simply ensure you build sufficient rapport with them before the end of the conversation.

Simple summary of step 4

Don't forget to chat:

- Arm yourself with conversation topics.
- Find out what the other person is interested in, and talk about that.
- How can I help this person?
- Interested, not interesting.

Step 5 – Get out of the conversation

Have you ever been stuck with someone at a networking event? It's such a terrible feeling. It makes you feel so helpless – there's nothing you can do. You're conscious of the 3-4 times you could have stopped the conversation earlier, but didn't. And now there's no easy way to wrap things up.

You want to be polite and behave with integrity. You want to continue the professional, interested, interesting approach you've taken so far. But – as your world comes crashing around you – you end up blurting out, 'I'm terribly sorry, but I really need to go to the toilet'!

The number of people who finish a conversation in a networking event with either 'I want to go to the toilet', or 'Excuse me, but I need a drink' is astounding. It's amazing that, in this day and age, we come across so many adults with their own businesses, families, houses, cars, children … who can't control their liquid, either going in or out!

So, we need to finish the conversation in a different way…

Getting their business card (if you want it)
Ask yourself:

1   Are they a big fish, tiddler or boot?
2   Do you want their contact details?
3   How can you wrap the conversation up?

You will already know if they are a big fish, tiddler or boot, so point 1 is covered.

For point 2, your actions will depend on the type of person you are speaking to. If you are speaking to a big fish, you must get their contact details.

The overriding rule with doing this is to always be polite (those good manners again) and ask at every stage:

- *Ask* if they are happy with you calling to set up a further meeting.
- *Ask* if you can have their business card, so that you have their contact details (and make sure you look at it when they give it to you – it is the height of rudeness not to).
- *Ask* if you can write on the back of their business card when you will be calling them. (Writing the day you'll call is very important: it shows commitment from you that you are going to call them.)
- *Ask* if they would prefer that you call on, for example, Thursday or Friday. (Don't say 'Shall I call on Thursday?'; they might say no! Give them a choice of two days, and then they can choose their favoured one.) Write this day down on the back of their card.
- *Ask* if they would like one of your business cards too; don't just give it to them.

Nobody could take offence with this approach. You haven't been pushy. You have behaved with respect, integrity and good manners. You haven't tried to make a sale.

Yeah, but ...

Question: What if they say 'No' to any of the above questions?

Answer: It is unlikely that they will. However, if they do, simply say 'OK, that's not a problem. I've really enjoyed speaking to you anyway. Enjoy the rest of your evening.'

If you are talking to a tiddler, it is not as critical that you get their business card, but it is still worth you having their details (for future marketing campaigns, invitations to events, useful contacts for your contacts, etc). Say you have enjoyed speaking to them and ask for their business card so you can put their details on file. Don't try to make an appointment for coffee, unless you really think it could be worth it.

For boots, it's totally different, because you might not want their card at all! (But, if they give it to you anyway, simply accept it with thanks …)

So, the end of the conversation is near. You have their business card (if you want it), with the promise of future contact if desired.

You've achieved all the goals of your networking event. You have the opportunity for a cup of coffee with a big fish. The event has been a success.

How to get away

You need to finish the conversation … without using the excuse of the toilet. There are all sorts of lines you can use to finish a networking conversation appropriately. One is: 'I've really enjoyed talking to you this evening.' This works well because the word 'enjoyed' is in the past tense (the inference being that the conversation is over). When you say this, the other person will invariably say, 'Thank you. I have too', to which you can respond with, 'Great. Enjoy the rest of your evening', and go your separate ways.

However, in my opinion, the absolute best way to finish a conversation uses information you discovered in step 2 …

Do you remember, the BIG QUESTION to ask when networking …

'What professions are good contacts for you?'

I told you that their answer would prove helpful in step 5. This is how ...

If, they said insurance salesmen would be good contacts, you could try the following as your closing lines:

> *You: 'Do you remember how you said insurance salesmen are good contacts for you?'*

> *Them: 'Yes.'*

> *You: 'Well, if I bump into any insurance salesmen this evening, shall I introduce them to you?'*

If you were the other person, you'd be delighted if you heard this. Their big fish are insurance salesmen, and you have just said that you are going to try and find some for them. They are bound to accept; in which case, say, 'Great, I'll do that. Thanks again for your time. I've really *enjoyed* speaking to you.'

Not only do you finish the conversation politely, the other person is also keen for you to go because you could well be able to introduce them to a big fish.

Simple summary of step 5

1 Establish if they are a big fish, tiddler or boot.
2 Get their contact details (if you want them).
3 End the conversation with an appropriate finishing line, for instance: 'You know how you want to speak to insurance salesmen? Well, shall I introduce you to any I meet this evening?'

If in doubt

My partner Emma is one of the best networkers I have ever seen. Although I teach this stuff, I marvel at the way she can move in and out of conversations, impressing everyone she speaks to, putting people together, treating everyone she speaks to with respect, and so on.

The reason she's so comfortable is because she has what she calls a 'host mindset'.

Emma thinks hosts are always the best networkers. I agree with her. They breeze in and out of conversations with ease. They introduce people to others. They don't mind approaching strangers. They can often be the most comfortable people in the room.

So, at every event she attends, she pretends she is the host. This helps her feel comfortable talking to anybody.

She finds this host mindset gives that extra inner calm you need to be able to speak to people in a relaxed, confident manner. And, as the old saying goes, 'You only get one chance to make a good first impression.' So, if pretending you're a host works for you, then do it.

Bringing it all together

Do you remember how I said networking is very much like driving a car? All the individual bits aren't too hard, but putting them together is much trickier, until you are used to it.

Fig. 4.6 summarizes and outlines all the main points you need to remember when working a room. Why not use this diagram as an *aide-memoire* to help make the most of any networking event you attend?

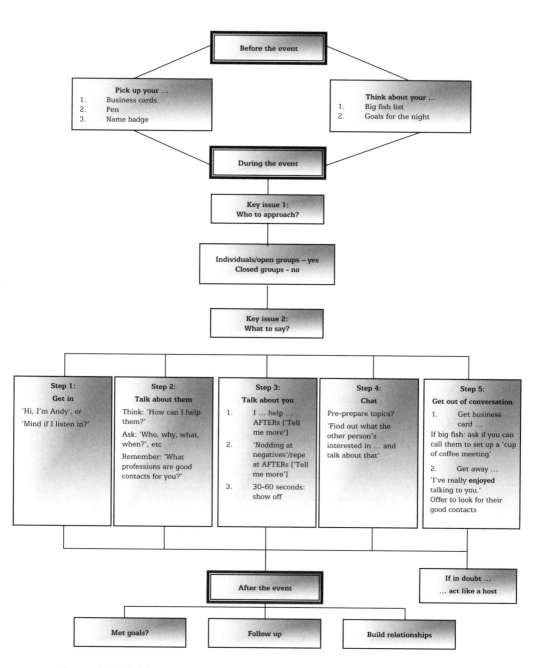

Figure 4.6 Working a room.

After the event

Without wishing to over-dramatise the importance of this section, if you don't follow the advice here, *every single thing* you've learnt about networking so far will be a complete waste of time.

During the event, you agreed with some big fish you'll be calling them to organise a cup of coffee. But, if you don't make those follow-up calls, the event will have achieved *nothing*.

Fortunately, follow-up is not hard to do:

1   Evaluate whether you have met your goals.
2   Follow up in the right way.
3.   Build relationships.

Looking at each in turn …

Evaluate whether you have met your goals

There is no point in setting a goal if you don't then check whether or not you've achieved it. Therefore, when driving home, ask yourself: 'Did I achieve my goal tonight?'

The following questions will help you see how you fared:

- Did I do what I set out to do?
- Did I meet the big fish I'd highlighted that were on the guest list?
- If I met my goals, did I set them too low? Should I set them higher next time?
- If I didn't meet the goals, why was that? Were the goals too harsh, or did I not perform as well as I could have done?

Doing this on the way home only leads to *positive* results. Either you will feel pleased you met your goals, or you will form an action plan in your mind for how to meet them next time.

Follow up in the right way

You've worked really hard to engineer a meeting with a big fish. You followed all the rules of networking. You've agreed with them that you can call on Thursday/Friday to organise a cup of coffee.

So you absolutely, positively *must* ring them on Thursday/Friday to organise that cup of coffee.

This can be nerve-racking. All sorts of thoughts can go through your mind: 'They were just being nice, they won't want to see me really', 'I'll bet they're too busy to hear from me', 'I've got a couple of reports to get out by the end of this week, so I'll ring them on Monday next week.'

But, you *have to* follow up. BNI's founder, Dr Ivan Misner conducted a survey of more than 2000 networkers in four different countries. They were given a list of traits of effective networkers, and asked to write which was the most important. And *'Following up* on referrals' outstripped all the others (including such things as having a positive attitude, being trustworthy, and being enthusiastic).

Effective networking is all about building productive business relationships; you *must* do what you said you would: ring the big fish on Thursday/Friday.

The call won't take long. All you are trying to achieve here is to get an appointment for a cup of coffee. Therefore, the script for your phone call can be very simple. It need only contain the following:

- a reminder of who you are and where you met;
- a reminder that it was agreed you would ring Thursday/Friday;
- a reminder they agreed that they would like to have a cup of coffee with you; and
- agreement on a time/date when you can have this cup of coffee.

There could be other topics discussed but this is all that *needs* to be covered. And the conversation could be over in as little as a minute. As long as you remember *the sole purpose of this conversation is to get an appointment in the diary*, you will not be on the phone too long.

A script you might like to follow:

- 'Hello Bob, it's Andy Bounds. I met you at the Institute of Directors evening on Monday.
- 'I told you I'd ring you today or tomorrow.
- 'Do you remember, at the end of our chat, we talked about meeting for a cup of coffee?
- 'Which day suits you best next week? Is Tuesday or Wednesday OK?'

There are of course millions of different scripts you can use for this conversation, but don't over-complicate it. You met the person at the event. You're going to have coffee with them next week. This call is merely linking the two together.

Build relationships
The grass is greener on the other side (... or is it?)
Have you heard this phrase before? It means that what you're *not* doing always looks better than what you *are* doing. So, if you're bored with your job at X Ltd, you'll think, 'I wish I worked for Y Ltd.' Of course, when you get there ...

When BNI's founder Dr. Ivan Misner and I were having dinner following our presentations at a conference in Kuala Lumpur, he said this great phrase to me:

> 'The grass isn't greener on the other side. The grass is greenest where you *water* it.'

Of course, he's right. When you're networking, it's very easy to flit from person to person, like a social butterfly, and not really develop any lasting, productive relationships. You could join BNI for six months, think, 'This isn't working, so I think I'll go where the grass is greener and join the Chamber of Commerce.' Three months later: 'This isn't working, so I'm going to go where the grass is greener – I'm going to try the Institute of Directors.' Three months later … and so on.

But Ivan's contention is that you will get the most out of relationships that you water, nurture and develop. So, when you have your cup of coffee with this big fish, it's important to see it as the *beginning* of a long-term relationship. A relationship that will need continual watering to make it as green as it can possibly be.

To do this, do *everything* in your power to *help* the other person. When you have the coffee with them, ask how you can *help* them. Maybe invite them to another networking event you're attending that they didn't know about. Give them some free advice. Point them in the right direction in an area they're unsure about. It doesn't matter. Just do something – *anything* – that will help them.

Because that is what developing relationships is all about. You both have to help each other. So it's sensible for you to help first.

In 2004, I attended a conference in California, and I was blown away by one of the speakers – Niri Patel. He was brilliant. The audience loved him. He had a truly rousing standing ovation. The audience broke out into spontaneous rounds of applause at least ten times during his one-hour presentation. I actually felt it a privilege to be there and see him speak. In many ways, it still goes down as one of the best presentations I've ever seen in my life.

I didn't know Niri at the time. I'd heard of him, but no more than that. But, after hearing him speak, and having been helped so much by his content, I wanted to 'help him in return'.

So, I wrote him a testimonial. In it, I said my job was to help companies get results from presentations. I'd travelled the world speaking at conferences. I'd helped a lot of very large companies make a lot of money. But, in all my time as a presenter, he had delivered the best presentation I had ever seen.

Niri wasn't expecting anything like this – after all, he didn't know me, and I was just one of his audience of 250.

But he was really grateful. He asked how he could help me. I told him I hadn't done it for any help in return, I just thought it was the right thing to do. And we left it at that.

A short while later, Niri asked me if I would run a workshop for his customers in Yorkshire. I accepted. The day went extremely well, and gave me some great publicity (we also recorded a DVD of the event and subsequently sold thousands of them). It really got me noticed in his region.

I then introduced Niri to some people I thought might be useful to him, which resulted in lots of business for him.

By now, we had become very good friends. My children love his little daughter, Hollie. Our partners, Emma and Catherine, have become very close.

But, there was something I didn't know about Niri when I first met him … he is one of the world's leading authorities on nutrition. I saw him at the beginning of last year because I was 36 years old, weighed 280 pounds (127 kg) and was concerned about the fact that I couldn't shift this extra weight. It was taking a toll on my health and my energy levels. As Niri described it, I was 'vertically ill'.

Then, for the first time in my life I suddenly realised the mindset I needed to have to lose weight. I did everything he said. To the letter.

And, 18 months later, I've lost a third of my body weight, and people find it hard to believe that I was ever even overweight.

But I *was* overweight – for 36 years – which is over 95% of my life. It was Niri's help, guidance and support that kickstarted the weight coming off.

And I'll be eternally grateful to him for this. When I used to be over-weight, I never really minded too much – after all, you can eat and drink what you like if you weigh 280 pounds! But something must have felt not right, or I wouldn't have wanted to shift it.

But the strangest thing of all is that I might not have lost this weight if we hadn't become such good friends. And we might not have become such good friends if I hadn't written that testimonial for him all those years ago.

So, it just goes to show, you *never* know where helping someone will get you.

Some quick, random thoughts to improve your networking ...
Stand up straight
Body language is the largest component of the first impression you give. So it's important you look confident ... even if you don't feel it.

Ever heard the saying 'If I see crumbs on the in-flight table, then I know the wings are about to fall off the plane'? Well, poor body lan-guage can have the same effect! There will be some people who, if you look nervous as you approach them, will assume that you're rubbish at your job. Clearly unfair, but it happens.

So, make sure you get the basics right:

- Maintain eye contact.
- Stand as tall as you can.

- Stride purposefully.
- Smile.
- Maintain 'chin contact' (make sure the angle of your head looks right – if your chin is pointing downwards, you look nervous; if it is pointing upwards, you look arrogant. Ensure there is an imaginary straight line between your chin and the chin of the person you are speaking to).

How long should you spend with each person?

Earlier on, you saw how important it was to set goals. If your goal is to meet five strangers, and you are only at the event for one hour, you can't spend more than 10–12 minutes with any one person, or you won't meet your goal.

So, limit yourself to a maximum of ten minutes per conversation. Any less and you probably won't have made enough of a connection; any more and one/both of you will wish the conversation had finished sooner.

When should you arrive at an event?

If an event runs from 6pm to 8pm, should you be there at 5.45pm, so you're one of the first, or get there later, maybe 7pm?

Being there early helps you become a host. You feel more comfortable speaking to people as you welcome them into 'your' room. Also, you don't have the problem of turning up later, and entering a room where people are already engaged in conversation.

However, the first few minutes of an event can be fairly chaotic. Lots of people running around, trying to make as many connections as possible. Also, and this might just be me, but I seem to attract a large proportion of boots in the first ten minutes. You know the type of person … they shove a business card in your face, tell you what they do, ask if you want to buy from them, and then lurch over to their next victim.

If you are new to networking, it's probably best to get there early, since it's less nerve-racking than entering a crowded room.

However, if you've been doing it for a while, it might be worth hanging back and avoiding the early run-around.

Copy from the best

The simplest way to master anything is to watch a master. Want to be good at golf? Copy Tiger Woods. Therefore, identify someone who you know to be good at networking and ask them what their top tips are.

Be careful when you choose – these people often don't understand why networking is hard for others, because they find it so natural. So, they may be dismissive of how hard it is for you.

In my experience, the best person to speak to is somebody who *used to* find networking hard but now finds it easy, because they can tell you the learning process they went through to become good.

I first noticed this phenomenon in my early twenties when my desk was always a mess. No matter what I tried, it was always a tip. Papers everywhere. Piles of files I didn't need. Chaos. I just could *not* work out a way to keep it tidy, even though I knew I should. I spoke to a number of people about it. But I made the mistake of asking people who were naturally tidy, so they would say, 'Well, just tidy it.' Not very helpful.

The person who helped me turn this around was a lady whose desk had always been an absolute mess in the past. But, over time, she had mastered some techniques to make it easier to keep tidy. I followed her learning process, and I now keep a tidy desk all the time.

So, choose your networking advisor carefully. Find someone who will sympathize with your feelings, not make you feel worse.

What should you wear?

This completely depends on the event. As a general rule, it's better to be slightly overdressed than underdressed. So, if in doubt, smarten up! Better still, ask the host whether a suit or casual business clothes would be more appropriate. I even once saw a gentleman turn up at an event in a dinner jacket and bow tie! As it happened, he was going on to another event that evening, but – when I first saw him – I thought he was the doorman.

In BNI, where they are experts at telling people how to network, their advice is to dress as if you were seeing your most important client. So, if you're a builder, this doesn't mean you need to put on a three piece suit, but you would wear your best workgear.

How drunk can you get?

Believe it or not, this is one of the questions I am regularly asked. This could be because I speak a lot in the UK, where beer is a national pastime. But, there's a really simple answer to this …

Always drink less than everybody else.

So, if everybody else is drinking three glasses of wine, there's no harm in you having two. However, having five and bursting into song is not going to help your cause.

The best bet though is to drink *nothing*. It's safest …

Handling your nerves

Steve Evans is one of the nicest people I've ever met. I first met him at a conference I was speaking at in 2005. We got chatting during the break and he's a fascinating guy. He represented Britain in the Olympics as a swimmer, did a sponsored bicycle ride from St Petersburg to Moscow, and is a Toastmaster of some repute. He ran a thriving piano-tuning business for over 20 years.

Steve is also blind.

When I first saw him, he was standing alone, with his guide dog Taz, at the side of the room. After getting past Taz's enthusiastic welcome. Steve told me about his new coaching business – *Your vision, our insight* (isn't that a fantastic name?) – and how he uses his unique perspective on the world to help his clients improve their levels of customer service, by focusing on what customers *hear* when they enter your premises.

Since our first meeting, I've got to know Steve and his lovely wife Catherine very well. They have become good friends. During a recent conversation between Steve and me, I asked what it's like for him to go networking.

I know from my conversations with my Mother that blind people rely a lot on sound to get their bearings. But, as you and I know, networking events are a mass of sound, which I would expect to be very disorienting for a blind person. Also, a lot of my content in this chapter has focused on which groups to approach, and how you should maintain good eye contact and so on, none of which you can do if you're blind.

Steve said something that I found really interesting. He told me that, when he first started networking, he had this irrational fear that, when talking to somebody, they might walk away while he was speaking. And he wouldn't know they'd gone since he wouldn't be able to hear it.

This greatly troubled him, so much so that he really didn't want to attend networking events for fear of it happening.

It was his wife Catherine who helped solve this problem for him, by saying: 'Well, Steve, if people are going to be that rude, there's nothing you can do about it. You just have to trust that people don't behave that way. And, if they do, they're really not worth your time anyway.'

And this was all the advice Steve needed. All of a sudden, he knew that the worst that could happen to him would be that a rude person disappeared out of his life, which isn't that bad at all.

Since then, Steve has attended – and flourished at – many networking events. He's done so well that he now sets up his own networking groups, teaching other people how to network.

I think it's fair to say that Steve has overcome his number 1 fear when networking!

Now I don't know about you, but this story touched me. I know that I would *never* walk away from a blind person when they were speaking to me. You know you would never do that. In fact, I imagine that you and I don't know *anyone* who would be rude enough to.

But, although we know what Steve was fearful of won't actually happen, that doesn't make his fear any less real for him.

And I used to experience a similar thing. When I weighed 280 pounds, I sometimes would feel nervous entering a room because I thought people would think 'he's fat'. But, do you know, I don't think they ever did. I think they just thought I was a nice guy who was interested in helping them.

So, our fears are very real to us, but they're not always worthy of our time.

The fizzy drink Dr Pepper has a slogan which says 'Dr Pepper … what's the worst that can happen?' To me, this phrase sums up how you can overcome your fears about networking. In Steve's case, his fear was that someone would walk off when he was speaking. But when you ask, 'What's the worst that can happen?', you realise the worst isn't that bad. If someone rude disappears, how does that affect your life? It doesn't.

Similarly, if someone thought I was too fat to speak to, 'What's the worst that can happen?' – nothing. If someone was going to think like that, or walk away from a blind person mid-sentence, surely that – more than anything else – would put them in the boot category, whoever they are.

To handle your nerves, construct a Dr Pepper table (Table 4.3):

My big fears	'What's the worst that can happen?'

Table 4.3 Dr Pepper table

List on the left hand side all the things that concern you, and write what the *worst possible* implications are on the right.

Worried that, after asking someone about their business, they won't ask you about yours? Well, the 'worst that can happen' is they have been very rude, you've identified another boot, and you've wasted four minutes of your life asking about someone who you probably won't speak to again.

Not too bad really, is it?

This Dr Pepper table helps identify, and immediately remove, your worst fears about networking.

And, don't forget, pretty much everybody is nervous when networking. So you're not alone if you feel awkward sometimes.

ENSURING YOU ARE IN THE RIGHT ROOM

On page 23, I told the story of George and Mary. George had tried to buy Mary some jewellery from a book store.

The purpose of the story was to emphasize the utter pointlessness of looking for thing A in a place that contains only thing B. And, just as you won't find jewellery in a bookstore, you won't find any lawyers at an event which doesn't have any lawyers in it. To work a room effectively, you have to be *in the right room,* one which contains your big fish.

When I used to be an accountant, we used to have our 'accountants' joke':

Accountants' joke

Question: Why did the accountant cross the road?

Answer: Because he did it last year.

All right, it's not the best joke you've ever heard. But, for accountants, that's as funny as we get.

But, just like the accountant in this joke, business people often go to the same type of networking events over and over again, even if they have never previously met any big fish at them. Yet they *keep* going. 'Because we did it last year.'

So, if we assume you want to meet lawyers, simply find where lawyers hang out. For instance:

- Law Society events;
- trade events;
- annual dinners;
- networking clubs;
- technical briefings, legal updates, etc.;
- policy meetings;
- bars/restaurants which lawyers frequent; or
- ask any lawyer you know where all lawyers hang out.

Then, get yourself invited to as many of the above as possible. Also, before attending any multi-profession networking events – like Chamber of Commerce – contact them and ask if lawyers tend to attend their events.

Simple summary

- Stop attending events that, based on past experience, are unlikely to provide business/contacts for you.
- Start networking at events frequented by lots of your big fish.

SO, WHAT NOW?

This whole section is *crammed* with information. As I was writing the book, I carried on asking myself, 'Is this section too long?' But I just couldn't see what I could cut out. Every single page contains simple techniques that you can apply so that you can grow your business by attending networking events.

But, when there is so much to take in, it's very easy to be overwhelmed by it. And, of course, that will lead to taking nothing on board.

The easiest way to use this section to grow your business through networking is to revisit the summary on page 22 – put everything into practice … and watch those big fish roll in!

How to sell more

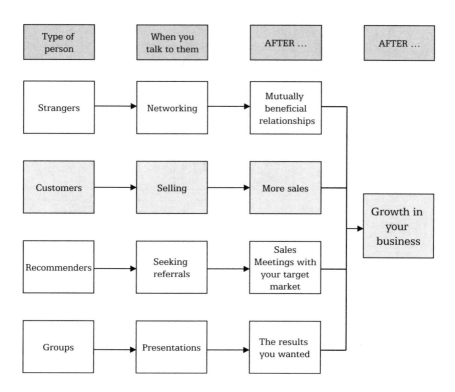

Type of person	When you talk to them	AFTER ...	AFTER ...
Strangers	Networking	Mutually beneficial relationships	
Customers	Selling	More sales	Growth in your business
Recommenders	Seeking referrals	Sales Meetings with your target market	
Groups	Presentations	The results you wanted	

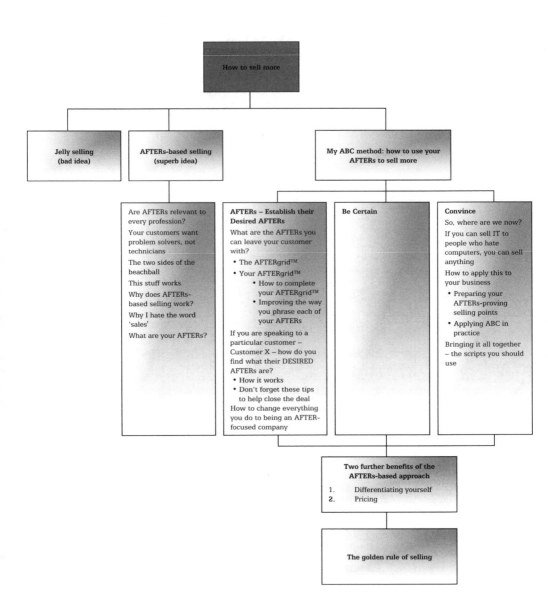

How to sell more

Jelly selling (bad idea)

AFTERs-based selling (superb idea)

My ABC method: how to use your AFTERs to sell more

Are AFTERs relevant to every profession?

Your customers want problem solvers, not technicians

The two sides of the beachball

This stuff works

Why does AFTERs-based selling work?

Why I hate the word 'sales'

What are your AFTERs?

AFTERs – Establish their Desired AFTERs

What are the AFTERs you can leave your customer with?

• The AFTERgrid™
• Your AFTERgrid™
    • How to complete your AFTERgrid™
    • Improving the way you phrase each of your AFTERs

If you are speaking to a particular customer – Customer X – how do you find what their DESIRED AFTERs are?
• How it works
• Don't forget these tips to help close the deal

How to change everything you do to being an AFTER-focused company

Be Certain

Convince

So, where are we now?

If you can sell IT to people who hate computers, you can sell anything

How to apply this to your business
• Preparing your AFTERs-proving selling points
• Applying ABC in practice

Bringing it all together – the scripts you should use

Two further benefits of the AFTERs-based approach
1. Differentiating yourself
2. Pricing

The golden rule of selling

JELLY SELLING (BAD IDEA)

*If you think hiring a professional is expensive, try hiring an
amateur.*

Red Adair

Business people say far too much irrelevant stuff. They fling jelly at
their audience, hoping some of it sticks.

And, you'll never see as much irrelevant jelly as when you see people
selling.

You'll have been on the receiving end of this yourself, as you sat through
suppliers flinging all sorts of information at you. And, sad to say, you'll
probably be guilty of it yourself. After all, everyone else is.

To show what I mean, imagine you're buying a website from a local
web designer. You invite them round to your office and ask the question, 'What do you do?'

They answer in the typical salesman's way – chronologically. In other
words, starting with who they are, and then building up to what they
do. Look at these eight sentences they might say:

1   'We produce websites for our clients'
    which means
2   'They have a presence on the internet'
    which means
3   'They have an increased profile worldwide'
    which means
4   'Potential customers are more likely to hear of them'
    which means
5   'Potential customers are more likely to be impressed (because of
    our fabulous websites)'
    which means

6   'They look better than their competitors'
    which means
7   'Potential customers are more likely to buy from them rather than
    their competitors'
    which means
8   'Their sales go up.'

A perfectly logical sales argument. But there's lots of jelly. I mean, wasn't it boring to start with? 'We produce websites for our clients.' You know this already, and it's not going to make you want to buy.

But read the eight sentences again, and ask yourself: 'If I was a potential client, which would be the most interesting one to me?'

There's a good chance it's number 8 – about sales increasing.

And which is the second most interesting? Number 7? The fact that potential customers are more likely to buy from you than your competitors?

In fact, if you were to write the above eight sentences in order of *interest to you* – the customer – it is highly likely that number 8 would be most interesting; number 7, the second most interesting; number 6, the third most interesting … and so on. The *least interesting to you* is the *first one* that was said. 'We produce websites for our clients.'

To *them*, what they said was in a sensible order – it was chronological But, to you, it was 'chron-*illogical*'. The order didn't make sense. The first words out of their mouths were boring jelly. It only got interesting later.

When you sell, are you the same as this website company? In answer to potential customers asking 'What do you do?', do you fling any of the following in your first 1–2 sentences:

• what you do;
• your date of incorporation;
• your number of offices;
• your staffing levels;

- your product range;
- a comment about your strong technical expertise;
- your track record; or
- your company's mission statement?

I guess you do. When I created my sales programme *Win that Pitch*, I found the *vast majority* of sellers did.

But it isn't captivating to your potential customer. And you don't want the first words that come out of your mouth – *the first impression you give* – to be of someone flinging jelly. Instead, you want the most relevant and interesting things first. So, the website company would do better saying their previous eight sentences *in reverse*:

- 'We can help improve your sales'
  because
- 'We make potential customers more likely to buy from you than your competitors'
  because
- 'We make you look better than your competitors'
  because
- 'We make you look more impressive to your potential customers because of our excellent websites'
  because

… and so on.

In other words, start with the *end result* first. The website company is now telling you what you'll be left with AFTER your work together (more sales), not what they do (websites).

And this is the crux of selling. The centre point.

> The most interesting, most important, most *critical* fact to tell a customer … is what they will be left with AFTER you've done your work.

AFTERS-BASED SELLING (SUPERB IDEA)

I've mentioned elsewhere my selling programme *Win that Pitch.* Fig. 5.1 and Fig 5.2 are taken from it and show why AFTERs are so critical in selling, and why they work:

Module 7
What customers are *really* buying – is it financial or emotional?

7.1 The AFTERs

"But amazingly, only a very few, very smart salesmen realise its power and exploit it fully in their sales pitches."

Now you've established your buying points in Modules 1–6, it's time to look at something *even more powerful*: the AFTERs.

"AFTERs" is an expression I've coined, but you may have heard the idea in another form elsewhere.

I'm talking about the difference between features and benefits. Good advertisers always use this idea when they focus on what a product *does* for someone rather than what it *is*. But amazingly, only a very few, very smart salesmen realise its power and exploit it fully in their sales pitches.

So why are "AFTERs" so important…?

The answer comes in one devastating sentence:

"Customers don't care what you do;
they only care what they're left with AFTER you've done it".

I suggest you read the sentence again. Think about it. Do you agree?

"My close rates rocketed. My clients' close rates rocketed."

When I first devised this sentence, it transformed everything. My close rates rocketed. My clients' close rates rocketed.

So how does it work? Well, think about any product – say your daily newspaper. You didn't buy it just because you wanted sheets of paper with the news printed on them. You wanted the *knowledge* you'd get AFTER reading that print, or the gossip, or your horoscope, or the TV programmes, or the weather report – whatever mattered to you.

ANDY BOUNDS

win that pitch

Figure 5.1 *Win that Pitch* module 7, page 2. www.andybounds.com/winthatpitch

Bought a lamp? You wanted *light*.

"Every single product is bought because of what customers are left with AFTER they've bought it."

Toothpaste? Clean *teeth*.

A pair of glasses? Better *vision*.

Contact lenses? Better vision without anyone knowing you're short sighted.

And do you know the weirdest thing? You could have sworn you wanted to buy a newspaper, a lamp, some toothpaste, a pair of glasses, or contact lenses.

Every single product is bought because of what customers are left with AFTER they've bought it (even though they don't realise it necessarily).

As US business school professor Theodore Levitt famously said, "People don't want 1/4 inch *drills*. They want 1/4 inch *holes*".

All this is simply a simpler way of looking at features versus benefits. When you think about it, features are what you do; benefits are what your prospect is left with AFTER you've done what you do.

"When you say the word 'benefit' in a pitch, your prospect is most likely going to think 'Here we go – here comes the sales pitch'. "

And I find "AFTERs" a more helpful term than "benefits" for two reasons:

1. It forces you to think about the *future good of the client*, which is the only true way *they'll* see a benefit in what you do, and

2. When you say the word "benefit" in a pitch, your prospect is most likely going to think "Here we go – here comes the sales pitch", because many of them know you've been taught to sell using the word "benefits".

So, let's see what your customers/prospects are really buying from you. What are they left with AFTER you've worked for them? Complete the left hand column of the **AFTERtable™** below (produce at least five points, ten would be great).

Figure 5.2 *Win that Pitch* module 7, page 3. www.andybounds.com/winthatpitch

Are AFTERs relevant to every profession?

Well, let's see. Table 5.1 gives a list of professions, together with some of the AFTERs they leave their clients with.

Profession	AFTER working with [this profession], clients are left with ...
Accountant	A larger, healthier business; smaller tax bill, etc.
Marketing company	Increased sales
Telesales	More sales appointments
Printer	Contacts who are impressed (by your brochures, letterhead, etc.)
Business coach	Increased company value; more time with your children
IT Trainer	Staff time freed up
IT installation	Time saved; less hassle; increased profits through greater efficiency
Architect	A building you are proud of, that meets your needs
Nutritionist	More energy; thinner/healthier weight
Life coach	Being the best you can be, and proud of your achievements
Recruitment	The right people in place to take your business forward
Financial planner	Your money working for you, not you working for your money
Health insurance	Your children and loved ones protected and safe
Barrister	Not being in jail
Banker	The resources you need to move forward
Graphic designer	Improved profile and image of your company, to increase sales
Conveyancing solicitor	The house of your dreams/business premises you need
Motivational speaker	Improved company performance, increased productivity of staff
PR company	Increased sales, profile

Table 5.1 Various professions and the AFTERS they give

Can you see how this works? Customers are interested in the right-hand column – the AFTERs. They want to pay less tax, buy their dream home, protect their children. They do not want 'an accountant', 'a conveyancing solicitor' and 'health protection'.

There is no doubt that Theodore Levitt's 'drills/holes' idea is true. But the strange thing is that, even though customers are ultimately interested in the AFTERs, very often *they are not even aware of it*. If *you* were the one who went to the hardware store and spoke to a *drill* expert about a *drill*, you would think you wanted a *drill*, even though it's the *holes* you're after.

And this is one of the totally weird things about sales and purchases. There is a *total lack of awareness* – from either side – that it is the AFTERs that drive everything.

Purchasers don't realise they're only ultimately interested in the AFTERs (they thought they wanted to buy a *drill*).

And sellers don't focus on the AFTERs, focusing instead on how great the drill is.

Similarly, when *you* sell, a large proportion of what you say will be focused on how great *your* drill is, and not the AFTERs your customers get.

So, *everyone* is focussing on the wrong thing.

For instance, when selling, do you – like most people – spend a lot of your time talking about:

- your selling points as a company;
- case studies of past clients where work has gone well;
- your product or service (maybe with a demonstration);
- industry statistics that support the need for what you do; and
- testimonials from happy clients.

It seems sensible to. But there is *no emphasis whatsoever* on the AFTERs you leave customers with.

Now, you could easily say, 'Yeah but … all the above selling points provide *evidence* that I can deliver fantastic AFTERs for companies.'

And that is no doubt true.

But, do you *categorically state* the AFTERs that they will be left with?

If not, leaving them to draw their own conclusions about the AFTERs you can deliver will never be as powerful as you stating them, and proving you can deliver them.

Your customers want problem solvers, not technicians

This title is a sentence you should remember. Customers don't want the best technical lawyer in the world. They want the lawyer who can solve all their problems.

So, to sell more, you have to be a fantastic *problem solver*.

And the first step of being a problem solver is to deliver fantastic AFTERs. You must leave *legacies of success* with every client you work with. And, then tell new clients the legacies they'll be left with AFTER working with you.

The two sides of the beachball

One of my good friends, Paul McGee, is a fantastic professional speaker. His book *SUMO – Shut Up and Move On* has changed the lives of thousands of people. He speaks all over the world, he is a Fellow of the Professional Speakers' Association (the highest accolade possible) and is well known on the speaking circuit as being at the very top of his game.

One concept Paul developed is that different people look at issues as they might look at a beachball. A beachball, as you know, has six coloured segments on it. They might be red, white, blue, yellow, green, orange. If you and I held the ball between us, the ball might look red, white and blue to me. However, from your side, you would think the ball was green, yellow and orange.

So, the *same* ball looks *completely different* from different perspectives.

Paul then goes on to talk about how this is true in many aspects of our lives. How two people can view the same thing in completely different ways. Like, *I* didn't think leaving a wet towel on the bed was a problem. But Emma …

Apply the beachball idea to selling. You look at your company – the beachball – from a certain point of view. You think of it as having lots of good selling points. You focus on what you think will persuade others to buy.

But, when your prospective customers hear what you say, they're looking at your company – the same beachball – from a different point of view. They want to see *evidence* you can provide the *AFTERs* they are looking for. And that's all.

This stuff works
The rest of this section will show you how to sell using AFTERs.

Apply the contents of this section to your business, and it will transform your results.

I know this because it has worked for *every single company* I have worked with, from multi-national blue-chips, to small Liverpool-based businesses; from charities looking to win national accounts, to family-run enterprises where more income literally means more food on the table that night.

One of my clients is Hubbub UK. They are a PR and marketing company who specialise in creating buzz around what you do, and getting you the attention you need to succeed in your target market. Hubbub is run by two Kiwis, Mark Sinclair and James Kirk (not the one from Star Trek!). They are both very talented men, as are their employees and associates, but – before working with me – they never quite got the sales their skills deserved.

I showed them how to sell based on AFTERs, using my ABC technique (page 104). And, since then, they have won *every single sales pitch* they have made. Not only that, but clients have signed up quicker than before, making their sales pipeline much more efficient.

And some of their sales successes have been really eye-catching. They won a huge contract with the New Zealand government, which resulted in them running an important campaign, including projecting a massive image against one of the tallest buildings in Central London. Their work was so impressive, it got media coverage on the other side of the world, and made front-page news of *PR Week*, and led the government's communications and marketing director to say their message had 'reached well over five and a half million people'.

Because of how powerful the AFTERs-based approach is, Hubbub also now get better results for their clients, build better relationships with their clients faster, they're hiring more staff, and they've moved to some swish new premises.

Now, all this is pretty impressive. But it becomes even more so when you realise that Hubbub is a small Bristol-based company. They have less than ten staff, they regularly pitch against huge marketing and PR agencies, with worldwide brand names. Yet they still achieved – and continue to achieve – this level of success.

That *cannot* happen unless you have a hugely efficient and effective sales message, which they now do.

It's based on their AFTERs.

But that's just one company. Another organization I work with – a major bank – won business from 18 sales pitches out of 18. Delegates from another bank who attended one of my courses increased their weekly sales by over 47% based on the AFTERs.

Chris Beadsworth, former Chief Executive of Siemens' spin-out Landis & Gyr UK Limited, asked me to write a sales pitch to their largest client British Gas, at a time when they were – in Chris's own words – 'dead in the water with them'. As a result of their AFTERs-based pitch, Chris said, 'We now work more closely with British Gas than ever before'.

Without boring you by listing thousands of examples, you can see this stuff works. Because there's lots of AFTERs and no jelly!

Why does AFTERs-based selling work?

Imagine a timeline when working with clients, such as Fig. 5.3.

Figure 5.3 Timeline showing your work with your clients.

Traditional selling focuses on who you are, what you do, how you work, and the service you provide.

In other words, it focuses solely on everything you do up to the end of your work (i.e. everything to the *left* of the **X**).

But, because clients want AFTERs – even though they're not always aware of it – to sell more, you must focus on the time *AFTER* the end of your work together, i.e. to the *right* of the **X**.

The complete opposite of what you're currently focussing on.

Do you remember the sentence 'clients want problem solvers, not technicians'? Well, technicians focus on how they work (left of the **X**), whereas, problem solvers focus on the *right*, saying, 'By the time I have finished, these are the problems I will have solved for you'.

Now, let me ask you a question. Would you buy from someone who was a technical expert, or from someone who you knew *without any doubt at all* could leave you in a better place *AFTER* you had worked with them?

The answer is a no-brainer. We must focus all our efforts to proving we can deliver great things AFTERwards, not jellying clients with details of how we'll do the job.

Why I hate the word 'sales'
I don't know about you, but I've always hated the word 'sales'. And lots of phrases which include the word drive me mad too – sales pitches, unique selling points, etc.

The reason I hate the word is because it is solely to do with us, and not the customer. It is *we* who are *selling*. So, the word itself is from *our* point of view not our customers, who are making *purchases*.

Therefore, instead of the phrase *unique selling points*, I much prefer the phrase *unique buying points* – the unique things about you that customers will *buy into*. This is more powerful than what *you* think will sell. For instance, a great *selling point* for me is that bank winning 18 pitches out of 18. However, the thing you're more likely to *buy into* is the fact that my Mother is blind, giving me a unique perspective on communication, which helps me show others how to succeed when they speak.

Similarly, I would rather not use the word *sales* when talking about sales! Instead, I much prefer the phrase *agreement to help*.

Let me explain. If you can find the AFTERs your client wants, and then *prove* you can help them achieve these AFTERs, such that they agree to buy from you ... you've both *agreed* you can help them. Yes, technically, you've made a sale, and they've made a purchase. But it's been much more consultative than that.

What are your AFTERs?
I once heard a story about someone who had three children. The eldest – a boy – is two years older than the other two, twin sisters.

So, the couple went from having no children to one child, and then – when the twins came – from having one child to three.

The father of the children said the biggest jump was having the first child. In other words, it was a bigger jump to go from none to one, than it was to go from one to three.

And I love this idea about 'none to one' being the biggest jump. Because, it's like that in so many walks of life. When you go on a diet, the biggest jump is your first healthy meal. Trying a new idea in business ... the biggest jump is the first time you do it.

The phrase 'none to one' appears a lot in this chapter, because it's very important from a sales point of view. You'll see why later.

But, for now, I want you to go from none to one with your AFTERs.

I would like you to think what AFTERs *you* leave your clients with. Can you think of anything? Do you leave them with more profits? More sales? Do you free up their time? Do you reduce the stress in their office? Do you make them happier?

Go from none to one now, by making a note of an AFTER you leave clients with.

Before you do, a word of advice: when listing your AFTERs, there is one rule. You must *exclude what you do* from your AFTERs sentence.

So, if you are a *website* company, you cannot say, 'AFTER coming to us, you will have a *website*'. Instead, you should be saying, 'AFTER coming to us, you will have more sales.' So, a *website* company cannot mention the word *website* in their AFTERs.

Go from none to one now. List some of the AFTERs you leave your clients with (you've already touched on this in both the AFTERs and Networking sections). We'll go into this in a lot more detail shortly, but let's do the hardest jump – none to one – before we do.

MY ABC METHOD: HOW TO USE YOUR AFTERS TO SELL MORE

There are two things your customers want when making a buying decision:

1   their DESIRED AFTERs; and
2   absolute *certainty* that you can provide them.

These are the only two things customers are interested in. If they know with 100% *certainty* that they will get the *AFTERs* they require, they will buy.

This turns traditional selling on its head, of course. Because standard sales stuff – like your date of incorporation – does not satisfy either of these criteria. It has nothing to do with their AFTERs. And it does nothing to transmit *certainty* that you can deliver them.

I've devised a three-step approach to selling, which I call my ABC Approach. It ensures both *AFTERs* and *certainty* are covered. It's really simple, but incredibly powerful.

The three steps to the ABC Approach are:

AFTERs – *establish* their DESIRED AFTERs;

Be certain – *state with certainty* you can provide those AFTERs; and

Convince – *prove* that you can deliver those AFTERs.

In other words, find out what they want, and then prove you can give it to them.

This approach will help you get the sales that someone of your expertise could – and indeed should – get.

Another good thing about the ABC approach is that you don't have much extra work to do. You will see that 90% of what you say in the ABC approach is made up of things you currently say when selling. So, although it's a totally new framework, you have not got much new material to find. What you *do* need to do is restructure how you say it.

Do you remember the five steps to communication that I outlined in section 3: 'AFTERs'? These are the five steps that my mother and I developed to make communication effective:

Always context first;

Frame of the other person;

Thoroughness is key;

Extra info; and

Required information only.

The ABC approach satisfies *all* five criteria. You will see it puts the sales meeting in *context* for the customer (rule 1), and that it's totally geared to being *in their frame* (rule 2). Detail is only given where it's needed (rule 3), you never give too much information (rule 4). And – crucially – the only words you say are relevant to the audience (rule 5).

In other words, *no jelly*. Not one wasted word. And every single thing you say impresses the client.

The rest of this section outlines how to use the ABC approach. My advice is this: for you to get best use of this section, every time I suggest you apply what I have just said to your business, break off from reading, get a piece of paper and write down your answers to the questions I raise.

That way, AFTER you finish reading this section, you will have your new sales process written!

AFTERS – establish their DESIRED AFTERs

The A of the ABC approach is concerned with establishing the customer's DESIRED AFTERs.

There are three elements to this:

a) What are the AFTERs you can leave customers with (in general)?
b) If you are speaking to a particular customer – Customer X – how do you find what their DESIRED AFTERs are?
c) How do you change everything you do to being an AFTERs-focused company?

You need the first of these to see the AFTERs your business is capable of producing.

The second helps you apply this info to Customer X, so you don't jelly them.

The third will help your business get the maximum sales possible.

So, let's look at each of these in turn, starting with:

a) What are the AFTERs you can leave your customers with?
The AFTERgrid ™

There are two types of AFTERs: business-related and emotion-related.

For instance, AFTER buying a computer system, your business processes will be more efficient (*business*-related AFTER) and your staff won't feel as frustrated as they did with the previous computers (*emotion*-related AFTER).

Similarly, we can also subdivide AFTERs into being either positive or negative-reducing.

So, in the previous example, increasing a company's efficiency is a positive AFTER (it takes the company forward); whereas reducing staff frustration is a negative-reducing AFTER (it stops bad things continuing).

Putting all this together, you can construct your own AFTERgrid™ for the AFTERs you leave clients with:

	Business	Emotional
Positive		
Negative-reducing		

Table 5.2 Construct your own AFTERgrid™

Across the top, the two types of AFTERs – business and emotional; down the side, you will see that both types can be either positive or negative-reducing.

To make it clearer, let's go back to the example of the computer company. Here are some of the AFTERs they might provide for their clients, placed in the appropriate quadrant:

	Business	**Emotional**
Positive	• Greater efficiency • Increased profits	• More motivated staff • Staff pleased with the reports the new system produces
Negative reducing	• Your staff will stop getting bogged down in unnecessary processes • Eradication of the threat of computer viruses	• Less whingeing from the staff • Reduction in feelings of wanting to put your foot through the computer screen!

Table 5.3 Example AFTERgrid™ completed for a computer company

Can you see how this works? For instance, the top left quadrant – Positive Business AFTERs – shows how the new computer system will *drive the business forward* in terms of both increased efficiency and profits.

However, the bottom right quadrant shows the current negative emotional issues that the new computer system will resolve.

Your AFTERgrid ™

Earlier in this chapter, you wrote down some of the AFTERs you deliver (when you went from none to one, on page **xx**.) Why not find more of your AFTERs now, by:

- constructing a blank AFTERgrid™;
- inserting the AFTERs you currently have in the appropriate quadrants; and
- completing the grid?

You'll need *at least two* entries in each quadrant to ensure you can address whatever AFTERs a particular customer might seek.

Why not do this now and fill in Table 5.2, before reading on?

How to complete your AFTERgrid™
You should now have at least eight AFTERs, maybe more.

But to find *all* the AFTERs your company is capable of, here are two suggestions that will help:

Firstly, the best way to find what AFTERs you leave your *customers* with ... is to call your favourite *customers* and ask what AFTERs they got from you. (Incidentally, I have found an additional benefit of doing this: it reminds your customers how good you are as a supplier, because their AFTERs are spelt out to them. And reminding customers about your unparalleled excellence never does any harm!)

The second way to add to your AFTERgrid™ is to use a simple mnemonic that I created: the 'last RITES'.

RITES stands for five AFTERs that customers tend to want some/all of:

Risk reduction

Income increase

Time saved

Expenditure reduction

Stress relief

If your business is able to deliver these five AFTERs, but some are currently missing from your AFTERgrid™, simply insert them, in the appropriate quadrant(s).

Improving the way you phrase each of your AFTERs
The next step is to make your AFTERs as compelling as possible.

To do this, either get a partner – or have a conversation with an imaginary person – and use the following phrases:

You: [Read out one of your AFTERs.]

Them: 'Why should I care about that?'

You: 'Well, it's a good thing for you because …'

Using these sentences makes the *benefits* of your AFTERs much clearer. So, taking one of the examples from the computer company's AFTERgrid™, this is how it works:

You: 'Your staff will stop getting bogged down in unnecessary processes.'

Them: 'Why should I care about that?'

You: '<u>Well, that's a good thing for you because</u> they'll be able to focus on more productive work.'

Them: 'Why should I care about that?'

You: '<u>Well, that's a good thing for you because</u> they'll be able to increase your company's bottom line, rather than being tied up in resource-draining work which adds nothing to your business.'

Look at the bottom sentence. It's much more customer-centric.

Again, why not do this now, before moving on? After all, AFTER you've done it, you will have:

- a list of every single AFTER you can deliver …
- … phrased in such a way that it makes a very compelling sales argument.

**b) If you are speaking to a particular customer – Customer X
– how do you find what their DESIRED AFTERs are?**
How it works

What you've done so far is a great start but, if you flung *all* your AFTERs at a potential customer, there would still be too much jelly. Yes, it would be more interesting to them, but would still contain lots of irrelevances. They won't want half the AFTERs you can deliver.

To make sure you don't do this, you need to find the DESIRED AFTERs for every customer you speak to. And this is how …

When you go to a sales meeting with Customer X, after you have had the initial rapport-building, use some/all of these phrases to establish what her AFTERs are:

- What are you looking to achieve AFTER our work together?
- If everything were to go really well with this project, where would you be AFTER it?
- How would you judge this project to be a success?
- If you were to look back in twelve months' time, what would have to have happened for you to think this project had been a success?
- What disaster will befall your company if you can't get this sorted now?
- How will you feel if you can get this right?
- How do you measure if your business is doing well, and does this project improve these areas in any way?
- What keeps you up at night?

You won't use all of these questions, just one or two of them (until Customer X goes from none to one and tells you an AFTER they want from you). Then use these two words to move things along:

'Anything else?'

Once clients have said their first AFTER, the words 'Anything else?' draw more and more out of them.

In fact, you'll often find 'Anything else?' leads customers into telling you everything you need to know.

In my experience, when my clients hear the words 'Anything else?' for the first time, they ask, 'Is that it?' And, I admit, it doesn't sound very hard. But often in business it's the simplest things that make all the difference.

If I were you, I'd find your best friend in business and practise this questioning technique with them. Remember, you use one or two of the bullet-pointed questions above to get them going, and then say 'Anything else?' to draw a few more AFTERs out. You're not looking for millions here. Four or five will do.

Don't forget these tips to help close the deal ...
Here are a couple more ideas that will help you increase your chances of getting the sale for the price you want.

Firstly, if a client starts the conversation with a question to *you* – for instance, 'What do you do?' – you need to be able to deflect this or you'll end up talking about yourself first, and not them. This means you won't be able to ask them the questions outlined above. This in turn, will mean you won't know their AFTERs in time, so you'll start jellying them.

Where the client asks about you first, simply say, 'Thanks for asking, but the last thing I want to do is bore you with lots of irrelevant information about me. So, do you mind if I ask you a couple of questions first, to make sure I tailor what I say to you?'

This phrase is *impossible* for the customer to say 'no' to. Can you imagine them saying, 'No, be as irrelevant as you can. Throw your jelly at me. Fling away.'

And, secondly, to help with pricing (which is discussed on page 128), ask as one of your final AFTER-triggering questions: 'Excuse my ignorance, but what would these results be *worth* were you to achieve them?'

Again, customers don't mind answering this question because you've asked it from a knowledge-seeking point of view, and they're almost always happy to increase your knowledge by telling you. And, of course, once you know how valuable their AFTERs are *in their eyes*, subsequent discussions about pricing become much easier, because *they* can see the true value in what *you* will do.

Do you know, in my opinion, this section on AFTERs is the most trans-formational in the entire book?

Why? Because the devastating realisation that customers *don't care what you do* means you have to sell in an entirely different way from how the vast majority of people sell. And, using the questions out-lined above – like, 'What are you looking to achieve *AFTER* our work together?' – will help you find exactly what people *do* want to buy when they see you.

Understanding the *real* reasons why people should buy from you is the beginning of sales wisdom. It is the strong foundation of your sales argument; the firm platform on which you build all else.

Please, invest the time asking as many customers as possible what they think your AFTERs are. This will give you a more complete, realistic, customer-focused view of the AFTERs you provide.

And, of course, if you've agreed in advance on the criteria by which what you are doing will be judged (their AFTERs), and you are doing a good job, then you've got the start of a continuing series of sales … you're in business with Customer X for years.

I am frequently told by my customers, 'It was the AFTERs that did it, that won the business.' And this comment is usually followed by, 'I can't believe I didn't mention them before … or that my competitors don't mention them either!'

In a nutshell? Practise them. Use them. And watch them work.

c) How to change everything you do to being an AFTER-focused company

Since the AFTERs are so transformational, it makes sense to transform your whole business to becoming an 'AFTERs-producing entity'.

It is much better to be 'someone who helps clients' sales go up', rather than being 'a website company', or 'someone who makes people feel better' rather than 'a doctor'.

One time-efficient way to make a start with this is, when a customer is writing you a testimonial, ask them to talk about the AFTERs you left them with.

Most written testimonials are little more than glorified thank-yous – 'Thanks for the work you did. You did a great job.' Testimonials of this ilk are unlikely to lead to more work for you when you show them to potential new customers.

However, if you get a written testimonial starting, 'Since you worked with us, our company has improved by …', it provides *evidence to others* that your business is an 'AFTERs-producing entity'.

Since you are calling some of your customers anyway (to find what AFTERs they were left with from your work with them), why not add at the end of the conversation: 'I'm really pleased that the work we did has proved so helpful to you. Would you mind putting in writing what you just said? If you like, I can email over the wording you have just used for you to confirm?'

This kills two birds with one stone. Not only do you find the AFTERs you leave customers with, but – all of a sudden – you have a powerful AFTERs-rich testimonial that you can show to prospective customers.

But it's not just testimonials that can be improved. When demonstrating your product, devise a way of doing it which will show the AFTERs first. For instance, if Customer X is interested in saving time, start your demonstration with, 'Everything we do is designed to save time. For instance, when you press this ...'

And it doesn't stop there. If you use case studies to evidence your strengths, change the order in which you have written them. Practically every case study I have seen starts with the background of the client, then the work you did, and ends with the results – the AFTERs – of your work together.

Why don't you flip this completely? Start with the results you got – so your prospects can see the AFTERs straight away – then give the background information underneath.

And don't forget the best thing about all this ... your competitors won't have even *heard* of the mnemonic AFTERs.

After all, I made it up.

So, at the same time as you're using AFTERs-based selling to impress your prospects, your competitors are still flinging jelly at them, talking about all their products and services, and the fact they were founded in 1922.

And, although life isn't one big battle to smash competitors into the ground, the fact is, if you want to sell more, you *do* have to appear better than them. Or you won't make the sales you deserve.

Simple summary of the A in ABC

ABC stands for **AFTERs**, **Be** certain, **Convince**. To do the **AFTERs**:

- find Customer X's DESIRED AFTERs, by asking AFTERs-triggering questions, followed by 'Anything else?'; and
- change your marketing and selling messages to being totally AFTERs-focused (for example, starting testimonials with the word 'Since...', and so on.

Be certain

What men seek is not knowledge, but certainty.

George Bernard Shaw

The first phase of the ABC approach – establishing Customer X's DESIRED AFTERs – is the start of achieving the sale.

The second phase – the 'Be certain' phase – is very quick and simple: stating *with certainty* that you can help Customer X achieve the AFTERs she has just told you she wants.

I explained earlier how customers only seek two things when they are buying – AFTERs and certainty. This might have seemed strange when you first read it, but it's definitely true. You're like this yourself. For instance, if you are ill and go to the doctor, you want *certainty* she'll cure you. Speaking to a wedding photographer? You will want *certainty* you'll have your treasured day captured forever. A leaky tap? You'll want *certainty* the plumber will fix it.

From a selling point of view, George Bernard Shaw's quote can be changed to:

> *What customers seek is not knowledge (about your business), but certainty (that you can deliver their AFTERs).*

Although this 'Be certain' phase is critical, it doesn't take very long. In fact, it's *only two sentences*. It's by far the easiest of the three phases. But it's *essential*.

It links the first and third phases together by letting the customer know you've finished finding their AFTERs whilst giving them *certainty* you can deliver these AFTERs for them.

The two sentences are:

1   confirm their AFTERs (by summarising what they've just said); and
2   state with *certainty* you can deliver them.

An example of sentences you could use:

1   'So, am I right that you're looking for a computer system that will [here come their AFTERs …] free up your staff's time, so they can help increase your company's profits, by engaging in more profitable activities, whilst at the same time reducing the frustration they currently feel with your existing system?' [Yes].
2   'Well, I can *definitely help you* with this.'

And that's it. Just two sentences.

The first sentence is to put a line under the AFTERs part of your conversation by summarizing the key points of what they said. It also ensures you both have total clarity about the relevant issues.

The second sentence transmits *certainty* to the customer.

Note the phrase in italics in sentence 2: *definitely help you*. The word *definitely* is the powerful one here, because the customer sees there is no doubt in your mind whatsoever that you can help her. Without the word *definitely* (or a word like it), the sentence doesn't work nearly as well.

Now, although I am saying that this 'Be certain' phase is quite simple – after all, it is only two sentences – there are some words of warning that I must impress upon you:

• Only say *definitely* if you're *definite*. To say you can 'definitely help someone' when you are not sure you can, is lying and lacking in integrity. Remember, you're not trying to make a *sale* (that benefits only you); you are looking to make an *agreement to help* (which benefits you both).

- Be understated when using the word *definitely*. Don't make a big song and dance about, it, banging your hands on the table. Understated certainty works best. It's almost a shrug of your shoulders: 'Look, I can definitely help you. It's what I do.'

- If your profession is one such that you can't give certainty of an outcome – say, you're a mortgage broker who can't guarantee that the building society will grant your customers the mortgage they're after – make sure you're definite about something you can be definite about. So, you might say 'I can definitely put the best possible case to give you the maximum chance of getting this mortgage.' Or 'I'll give you a definite yes/no by Friday.' Don't make the mistake of promising a mortgage you can't guarantee.

- Although it is crucial, don't think certainty alone is enough to get you the sale. It's very unlikely you will say, 'I can definitely help you', and your customer will reply, 'Great – where do I sign?' The certainty sentences are simply statements which start the process of converting the sale.

The final thought for this section: one word to *avoid* during this phase is the word *try*. Often you will hear sales people say 'We'll *try* and sort this for you' and so on. But, when you think about it, the word *try* doesn't transmit certainty at all. In fact, it suggests doubt, the very opposite of certainty.

So far in this book, I have quoted some notable names – George Bernard Shaw, Red Adair, Drayton Bird and so on. But here are two more quotes from some less auspicious names, both of which convey exactly what I think about the word *try*:

*Do or do not. There is no **try**.*

Yoda, *The Empire Strikes Back*

And a second thought, given by a loving father trying to cheer up his children who failed at something they had recently attempted ...

> Well kids, you tried your best. And failed miserably. The moral of this story is ... never **try**.

Homer Simpson, *The Simpsons*

Remove the word *try* from your vocabulary when selling. Speak with certainty. After all, it's what customers want.

Simple summary of the B in ABC

ABC stands for **AFTERs**, **Be** certain, **Convince**. To **Be** certain:

1 'Am I right that you want ... [summarise their AFTERs]?'
2 'I can definitely help you ...'

Convince

So, where are we now?

Well your sales conversation is going really well. You have discussed their AFTERs for 5–10 *minutes* (the A phase), and then spent 5–10 *seconds* stating you can *definitely help* achieve them (the B phase).

A very productive chat so far – and you have not flung any jelly at anyone. Everything that has been discussed has been 100% relevant.

But it's now time to *prove* you can deliver the AFTERs you have just promised.

Remember, so far you have said nothing about what you do and how you work. It's now time to do so but, because your customer is now thinking in terms of their AFTERs ...

… you must relate everything you say about **your** business back to **their** AFTERs.

If you can sell IT to people who hate computers, you can sell anything.

Let me explain how to put your selling points in the context of customers' AFTERs by revisiting the example of our computer company on page 109. The AFTERs their customer wants are:

- more free time for their staff;
- increased profitability; and
- less frustration for their staff.

Let's say the computer company's traditional selling points (SPs) are:

SP 1   longest-established IT company in this city.

SP 2   Fastest-growing IT company in the entire region.

SP 3   Highest number of qualified staff (compared with other IT companies in the city).

SP 4   Excerpt from a testimonial from their Client A: 'We have measured our results since you installed our new system, and are delighted to say that you have saved our company 950–1000 man-hours per month. This equates to over £1m saving per year.'

SP 5   All our senior staff have chosen IT as their second career: they are *business people* first and foremost, and *IT people* second.

SP 6   Our company also has an IT training division.

SP 7   Our clients include the largest accountancy practice in the city.

In the eyes of our computer company, these seven selling points are pretty impressive. But, to read them as they stand ignores the customer's AFTERs they have just worked so hard to establish.

For instance, how does being the *longest-established IT company in this city* (SP 1) address any of the customer's AFTERs of saving time, increasing profits and reducing frustration?

Or how does the fact the computer company is the *fastest growing IT company in the entire region* (SP 2) impact on the customer at all?

It doesn't. So there is a very good chance the customer won't be interested.

This example shows why there is so much jelly flung by sales people. They think they're listing some great selling points, but customers feel they are on the receiving end of a barrage of irrelevant information.

But, if our computer company could develop these seven selling points such that they *proved* they could deliver the customer's AFTERs ... now *that's* powerful. And likely to lead to a sale.

The way to turn your *selling points* into *prove-you-can-achieve-their-AFTERs points* is by using the phrase you saw earlier in this chapter: 'Well, that's a good thing for you because ...'

So, if the computer company wanted to tie in *highest number of qualified staff* (SP 3) to the customer's desire to save time (AFTER 1), it might look something like this:

- 'We have the highest number of qualified staff.'
  Well, that's a good thing for you because ...
- 'They know the capabilities of IT more than less-qualified staff.'
  Well that's a good thing for you because ...
- 'If it is possible for some of your processes to be automated, our staff will be able to do this for you better than anybody else.'
  Well that's a good thing for you because ...
- 'Automating your processes means *your staff's time will be freed up* [i.e. AFTER 1].'

Make sense? It started off with a traditional jelly-rich selling point, with the selling company talking about one of their strengths. But, after development, it ended up with the selling point rephrased as a convincing argument proving they could deliver a DESIRED AFTER.

Let's have a look at another example, this time tying in the selling point *our company also has an IT training division* (SP 6) to another of the AFTERs:

- 'We have an IT training division.'
  Well that's a good thing for you because …
- 'We ensure you get the best out of your new system by training your staff straight away.'
  Well that's a good thing for you because …
- 'Your staff feel brilliant about the system from day 1.'
  Well that's a good thing for you because …
- 'It will *reduce your staff's frustration with IT* [i.e. AFTER 3].'

And so on. If you were to continue this, then group the revised selling points under the appropriate AFTERs headings, you would get something like Table 5.4 (page 124). In this table:

- The rephrased selling points are much more endearing to this particular customer than the original ones were, aren't they?
- One of the selling points (SP 6) appears in more than one of the columns. This does not matter. We want the best *evidence* for each AFTER.
- Two of the original seven selling points – being longest-established, and the fastest-growing in the city – did not make it to the table. This was because there was no obvious link between them and the client's AFTERs. However, if the computer company thought these SPs were crucial in helping transmit *certainty*, these points should either be (a) mentioned in passing during the discussion, or (b) be developed so that they do link into one of the above AFTERs – maybe, 'We are the fastest-growing IT company in the City (SP2), and this just wouldn't happen if we weren't good at

AFTER	More free time for their staff	Increased profitability	Less frustration for their staff
Rephrased selling points	• We know how to automate your processes better than any other IT company because we have more highly qualified staff (SP3). • We have a proven track record of success in saving time for our clients. For instance, client A said …(SP4). • We don't just leave you with a new IT system and let you get on with it. Instead we train all your staff how to use the system, so they get maximum benefit straight away, and don't waste time working out how to use it (SP6). • Accountants are judged on how well they use their time, so they would only employ an IT company that they knew would free up their time in the most effective way. Well, one of our clients is the city's largest accountancy firm, and they wouldn't have chosen us unless … (SP7).	• Our philosophy is firstly to look at your business, and then what systems you need in place to drive your profits up. • We then install the appropriate IT to ensure you succeed. • So everything we do is geared to increasing your profits. • We can take this approach because, before specialising in IT, all our directors were business people in their own right … (SP5).	• We ensure your new IT system doesn't frustrate your staff, by making it easy to use from day 1, because of the work of our training division (SP6).

Table 5.4 Revised selling points

knowing how to use IT to help *increase the profits of our clients.'* [AFTER 2]. Be careful though: don't jelly customers by forcing irrelevant selling points on them, just because you're proud of them. Some selling points are just not relevant.

How to apply this to your business

You need to rephrase your selling points into AFTERs-proving points if you're to impress customers. Obviously doing this on the spot, during a sales meeting, is hard to do.

So, you need to create a big bank of AFTERs-proving selling points in advance so that, when your customer says they want AFTERS 2, 5 and 7, you just say the AFTERs-proving points relating to 2, 5 and 7 only. No jelly. 100% customer-focussed. And both *AFTERs* and *certainty* are confirmed.

Preparing your AFTERs-proving selling points

You have already listed – in the AFTERgrid™ on page 108 the AFTERs you can leave a customer with. The final step in ensuring you're ready for your next sales meeting is to complete Table 5.5 (page 126) by:

1   putting each AFTER (from your AFTERgrid™) as a separate column heading;
2   developing each of your selling points using 'Well that's a good thing for you because', until they prove (at least) one of those AFTERs; and
3   transferring these improved selling points into the appropriate column(s) of the table.

AFTER doing this, you have – on one piece of paper – a list of all the AFTERs you can provide, plus all the supporting evidence you need to convince customers that you can deliver them.

	Transfer an AFTER from your AFTERgrid™ (page 108) here	Another AFTER from the AFTERgrid™ ...
AFTERs		
Rephrased selling points		

Table 5.5 AFTERs you leave your customers with – your new selling points

If I was going to recommend you do just one thing from the book, it would be to complete Table 5.5. Your sales will be transformed.

Applying ABC in practice

Earlier, during the A phase, you found the AFTERs that are important to that particular client. Let's say, of your eight AFTERs, they were interested in the AFTERs in columns 2, 5 and 7.

You then went through the quick B phase, stating with certainty that you can help them achieve these three AFTERs.

And now – to close the deal – you simply talk through the selling points that you have previously grouped under column headings 2, 5 and 7. Because these are your best chance of persuading the customer you can deliver their DESIRED AFTERs (2, 5 and 7).

And it really is as simple as that. You just find the AFTERs the client is interested in, state with certainty you can deliver them, and then provide all the evidence to convince them of it.

Don't forget, if you have eight AFTERs in your table, but the client is only interested in 2, 5 and 7, you do *not* mention anything in columns

1, 3, 4, 6 or 8. Why? Because it's not relevant to them. It's jelly. Don't fling it at them. They won't care.

Bringing it all together – the scripts you should use
Going back to our computer company, they have found the customer's DESIRED AFTERs – more free time, etc – and have stated with certainty that they could *definitely help*.

So to *convince* the customer that they can indeed deliver these AFTERs, they could:

1   Restate AFTER 1
    'The first thing you are looking to achieve is to free up some staff time.'
2   Restate *definitely* help you.
    'I know we can definitely help you do this because ...'
3   Go through the selling points which are relevant to this particular AFTER.

Simple summary of the C in ABC

ABC stands for AFTERs, Be Certain, Convince. To Convince:

1 Pre-prepare for the sales appointment by:
   • drawing up a table, with a separate column for each AFTER you deliver;
   • rephrasing your existing selling points so they become AFTERs-proving, by using the phrase: 'Well that's a good thing for you because ...';
   • putting these revised AFTERs-rich selling points in the appropriate column(s); and
   • learning them.

2 In the meeting, once you know the customer's DESIRED AFTERs, convince them you can help them achieve these AFTERs by going through your revised selling points **from the appropriate columns only**.

TWO FURTHER BENEFITS OF THE AFTERS-BASED APPROACH

Benefit 1 – differentiating yourself

You will be focusing on the fantastic *holes* you can leave the customer with. Your competitors will be talking about their *drills*.

So, your competitors won't be ABCing. They will be selling based on traditional lines (after all, pretty much everybody else does). Therefore, they look as if they are trying to make *sales*. You look like you are trying to make *agreements to help*.

Benefit 2 – pricing

It is much easier to deflect awkward questions about pricing.

For instance, how often do you experience this? You speak to a potential customer, they like what you do, they agree to buy from you … and then they ask if you can 'do anything about the price'?

The great thing about AFTERs-based selling is customers see where they're going to be in the future. And that is much easier for them to invest in, rather than simply giving money to you for a job you're about to do.

Many of my customers use AFTERs as a way to deflect pricing questions. But it's also one I regularly use myself.

Recently, a large organization asked me to speak at one of their international sales conferences. There were to be 1500 salespeople in the room. They asked me for a price. When I told them, they responded by asking if I could 'do anything about the price', saying, 'That's an awful lot of money for a one-hour talk'.

To this I replied: *'Yeah, but* … you're not paying for the hour, are you?

'What my talk will do will give *every single one* of your 1500 salespeople five new sales techniques they have never seen before, each of which will increase your sales. Not only that, but I'll phrase each one in such a way that they will be able to use them immediately after the conference.

'Therefore, you will have 1500 people, each using five new techniques the next day. That's 7500 new selling techniques your firm will have at their fingertips. The next day. And the day after that. And for evermore.

'These new techniques *definitely* work. And, the average value of one sale for your organization is over £10,000. So, AFTER your conference, your sales will shoot up.

'And *that* is what my fee covers. The extra sales you'll get.

'In fact, one thing I can guarantee is that your sales people *won't* make any sales *during* the hour I'm talking. Because they're sitting there listening to me! So, if you like, my fee covers all the future sales they will make. You can have my hour talk for free.'

My answer was met with the fantastic response: 'OK. That makes sense. Sorry for questioning it.'

So, I'd made an *agreement to help*. Both parties had agreed I could *help* achieve this firm's AFTERs: namely, that their sales people sell more.

But wouldn't it have been an easy mistake for me to try to justify my fee by majoring on what my talk would cover, my experiences to date, my client list and so on. But doing that makes it very hard to justify a lot of money for a one-hour talk.

THE GOLDEN RULE OF SELLING

The ABC approach is very simple. Establish what customers want AFTERwards, and then prove you can deliver.

But, despite its power, there is one rule of selling that overrides it. One rule that you must *never forget*.

You know when you visit a potential customer? The conversation goes well. They are impressed with what you do.

When this happens, the temptation is to *keep on talking* because they are enjoying what you have to say.

But, if you're not careful, you can talk yourself *out* of the sale. Have you ever done this? Most people have. And what started as an impressive discussion has ended up as a load of jelly.

The critical thing to remember when selling is the only thing you want from the customer is a 'yes'.

Once they have agreed to buy from you, there is no need to keep talking. Even if you haven't got to your main selling point yet.

So, the golden rule of selling is simple, but one that is very often forgotten:

When the customer says 'yes', SHUT UP!

You will find using the ABC approach gets to 'yes' much quicker. So, when you're in a sales meeting, go for the 'yes' rather than telling them everything you possibly can.

Finally, to answer the question you may well have been thinking as you read this chapter – '*Yeah but* … how long should I talk during the convincing phase?', the answer now is simple: until they say 'yes'.

And then you shut up!

Selling in this way is totally jelly-free.

You did not say one thing the customer didn't want to know.

You stopped talking when they wanted you to stop talking.

And, most importantly of all, you gave yourself the very best chance of getting a 'yes'.

Referrals

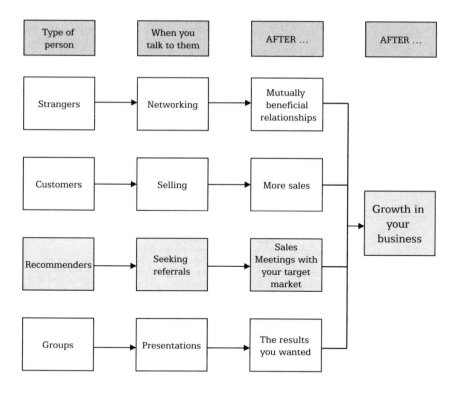

Type of person	When you talk to them	AFTER …	AFTER …
Strangers	Networking	Mutually beneficial relationships	
Customers	Selling	More sales	Growth in your business
Recommenders	Seeking referrals	Sales Meetings with your target market	
Groups	Presentations	The results you wanted	

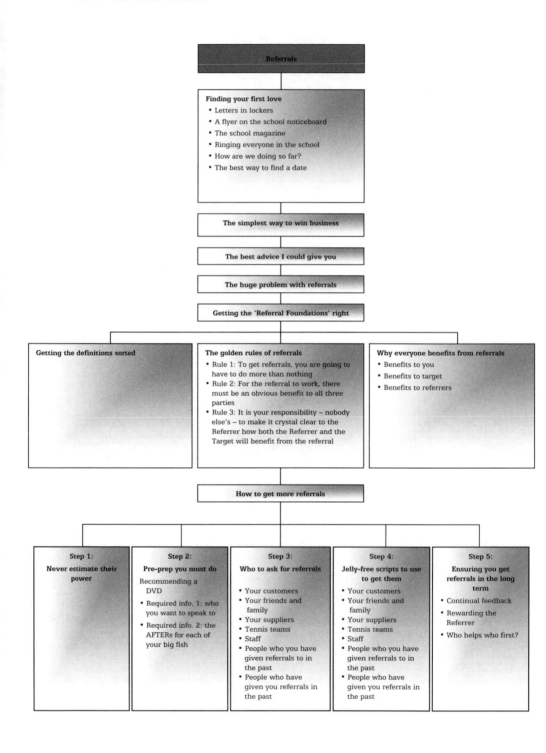

If you could only use one marketing method to win more business, what would it be?

I have always thought this is a great question. I mean, what would *you* do? There are so many choices out there – brochures, adverts, PR, cold calling, etc – all with advantages and disadvantages. But if you could choose *just one*, which would it be?

I find a really good way to think about this is to go back to your early courting days …

FINDING YOUR FIRST LOVE

Do you remember when you first became interested in finding a partner?

If you're anything like me, this was an exciting time, though nerve-racking. You don't know where to start. Who do you talk to? What do you say? How do you say it? What if they're just not interested?

Can you remember what you did to find a partner? Was it:

Letters in lockers

One way to strike lucky would be to write a letter extolling your virtues, maybe: 'I'm John Smith, in Form 11G. I'm good at sport, came top in maths and I like doing word puzzles.' Then, copy this letter hundreds of times, and put one in each student's locker, and wait to see what replies you get.

This might work – certainly, everyone in school would know about you – but, to be honest, it's hit and miss. You won't get many of the right kind of replies, if any. And it will have been expensive, and taken a long time to craft, print and post the letters.

I guess the best chance of success would be if:

- The person of your dreams …
- … is looking for someone like you …
- … at the *exact* time they read the standard letter you sent to everyone.

Not very likely.

And this problem is made worse by the fact that your letter is *bound* to contain irrelevant jelly. I mean, how is it possible to write a letter that is relevant and tailored to everyone?

No, we need to try something else. How about …

A flyer on the school noticeboard
Since the letter's not going to work, how about preparing a glossy flyer, and putting it on the school noticeboard where everyone will see it?

You could have a photo of yourself at the top, with you 'looking your best'. Underneath, you could write about why you'd be a good date. You could offer them an incentive to come along with you – maybe, 'I'll buy dinner. I'll even drive, so you can have a drink if you want to.'

You could even include a get-out clause for them: 'If you're not having a great time after the starter, you can go home there and then without any comeback from me'.

Again, this *might* work. People would see you in your best light. If no one else had a flyer on the noticeboard, or yours was the best flyer there, you would really stand out.

But the trouble once again is that the three things that need to happen simultaneously – the person of your dreams, looking for someone like you, *at that exact moment in time* – is very unlikely.

You could get no replies at all. You could get someone applying who's not:

- in the right age group for you;
- of the right personality; or
- of the right gender.

Obviously, you could improve your likelihood of success by putting the flyer where it gave you the best chance – maybe, the noticeboard in the senior girls' study room. But it's still hardly ideal.

There must be a better way …

The school magazine

If you know someone who contributes to the school magazine, why not pay them to write a gushing article about you, and what a great date you'd be? They could include flattering photos of you, maybe a couple of nice comments from people you've had previous relationships with: 'John was a great guy – I'd recommend anyone to go for dinner with him.'

This has all sorts of potential pluses – good exposure, people will know about you.

But, again, on a 'convincing scale' of 1–10 (where 10 represents someone being 100% convinced to go on a date with you, and 1 is someone who's not convinced at all), it's certainly not a 10. Even if the article was written superbly, it probably wouldn't convince someone *on its own* that they should go out with you. A great article might get you to a 6–7 on the scale, but you'd still have to do some convincing work when you met them to turn it into a 10.

No, no matter how impressive the article was, no one will date you just because of it.

So we're going to need something else …

Ringing everyone in the school
Maybe you could get hold of all your fellow students' phone numbers and ring each of them up in the evening.

You'd obviously practise the lines you'd say: 'Hi, I'm John Smith of 11G, and I've got a great opportunity for you. You know how you like having a good time? Well I have three evenings left in my diary this month, and I'd like to offer you the chance to …'

I can almost feel myself cringing at the rejection I'd get. Can you? It would be awful:

- 'Now's not the right time to call.'
- 'How dare you disturb me?'
- 'I'm having my tea.'
- 'How did you get this number? Never call me again.'
- 'Oh, I've heard of you, I don't think you and I would get on.'
- 'I'm not sure where you got this number from – I left that school three years ago.'

And these are just the polite things they might say.

So, this option would take hours of your time, and result in lots of aggressive negative responses.

How are we doing so far?
Very badly. None of the ways is ideal. All of them – the letter in the lockers, the flyer on the noticeboard, the magazine article, ringing

round the students – have real problems. They either contain irrelevant jelly, are expensive, time-consuming, lots of hassle or unpleasant to do.

And – most importantly – they're just not that likely to work.

The best way to find a date

I guess the simplest way is to:

1   Have a look around and find the person of your dreams (let's say, for this example, it's a lady).
2   Ask any of your friends if they know her.
3   If they do, ask them to put in a good word for you with her.
4   Once they've done that and she says 'I'd love to meet him', go and have a chat with her.

This is so much more likely to work:

- She's interested in hearing from you – after all, she's invited you over.
- She has a good impression of you before even meeting you.
- She first heard of you through a personal introduction.
- Some of her normal objections have gone – she's looking forward to speaking to you.
- She has a good idea that it's worth the two of you talking, so is more likely to be receptive.
- There's no jelly. The only words used to market yourself to her were 100% relevant to her.

To put it bluntly, it's more likely to *work*. And it's not jelly-filled, expensive, time-consuming, a hassle, or riddled with unpleasantness.

In fact, it's the opposite: relevant, cheap, quick, easy and pleasant.

So, if you could use *only one method* to get a date at school, it would – without doubt – be for your friends to recommend you to the person of your dreams. Every time.

THE SIMPLEST WAY TO WIN BUSINESS

And, now back to the question at the start of this section: 'If you could only use one marketing method to win more business, what would it be?'

The answer is now much easier. Because finding new business is very similar to finding love at school.

For instance, you can market your business by sending out brochures and mailings, just as you could extol your personal virtues with letters in lockers.

In fact, look at the similarities between the two situations (Table 6.1).

Marketing your business	Getting a date
Brochure/mailings	Letters in lockers
Advertising	Flyers on noticeboards
PR	Article in school magazine
Cold calling	Ring round everyone
Referral/personal recommendation	Your friends recommending you to the girl of your dreams

Table 6.1 The similarities between marketing your business and finding a date

So, brochure/mailings are like letters in lockers. They can work. They look fantastic and give your company a real feeling of worth, solidity, value. But – just like the letter – they're expensive, lots of them aren't read by the intended reader, and they often don't really *convert* sales. They're also, by nature, full of jelly. All the content won't be relevant to *all* the readers. On the convincing scale of 1–10, the most they will get you to is a 6–7 at best, but almost never a 10.

Compare this with cold calling. It can lead to a close (i.e. a 10 on the convincing scale), but there's also a lot of cases of 1. The take-up is often very low, and you have to deal with a great deal of rejection, abrupt replies and the phone being slammed down on you.

Advertising. Well, just like flyers on noticeboards, adverts can be very powerful (they must be, or the top 25 US advertisers wouldn't spend, on average, $45 billion annually domestically), but they won't *guarantee* a sale. And it's expensive.

> *I know that half of my advertising dollars are wasted ... I just don't know which half.*

> **John Wanamaker**
> **19th-century Philadelphia department store owner**

And PR (in our example, an article in the school magazine) – which can be so powerful – rarely gets 10 on the convincing scale on its own, especially if you're a small business, where good PR can be prohibitively expensive.

In fact, if we put the negatives of these five methods of winning business on a graph, it might look like Fig. 6.1.

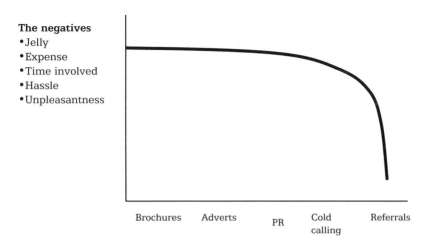

The negatives
- Jelly
- Expense
- Time involved
- Hassle
- Unpleasantness

Brochures   Adverts   PR   Cold calling   Referrals

Figure 6.1 The negatives of five methods of winning business.

Obviously, this graph is simplistic, and there's a good argument for a different order on the horizontal axis (you might feel the negatives of cold calling outweigh everything). But one thing is definitely true:

> Referrals have the least negatives.

Looking at the other side of the coin, Fig. 6.2 looks at the odds on *winning business* with each of the five methods.

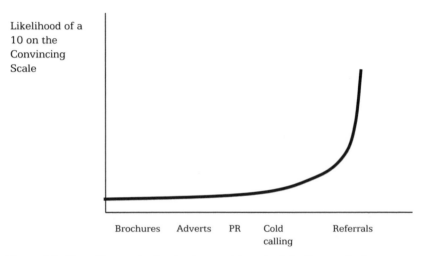

Figure 6.2 The odds on winning business with each of the five methods.

Again, very simplistic, and some of the horizontal axis could be moved around. But, one thing is definitely true:

> Referrals are most likely to win you business.

Combining these results (Figure 6.3) shows:

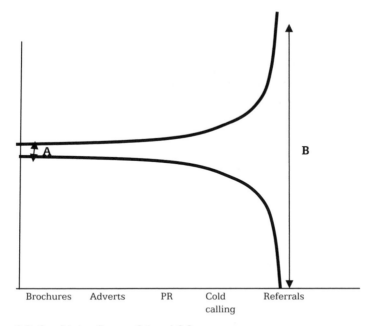

Brochures   Adverts   PR   Cold   Referrals

calling

Figure 6.3 Combining figures 6.1 and 6.2.

The net effectiveness (likelihood of sales less negatives involved) of each of the five marketing methods is shown by the distance between the two lines. As you can see, brochures (arrow A) are nowhere near as powerful as referrals (arrow B). In fact, the graph clearly shows that:

- Referrals have the least negatives.
- Referrals are most likely to increase your business.

And so, finally, the answer to my question at the start of this section is now easy:

Q If you could only use one marketing method to win more business, what would it be?
A *Referrals. Without question. Every single time.*

The best advice I could give you

The best website I've ever seen is www.draytonbird.com and it belongs to Drayton Bird. It's got 457 pages, answers 276 common marketing questions, has 52 short case histories and over 65 articles. Thousands of marketers all over the world use it. They stay on average for about 23 minutes (this isn't bad, since over half the people who visit a web site are on there for seconds only).

If I were you, I'd look at it. If the average time people spend there is 23 minutes, it must be pretty good. It has so much advice on there, on most forms of marketing, it's *got* to be worth some of your time. You'll receive marketing advice for free that you'd pay a lot of people a great deal of money to tell you. And you wouldn't know as much as if you'd gone to Drayton's site.

Now, a question for you: based on what I've just said, are you interested in taking a look at his site? I wouldn't be surprised if you are. Personal recommendations (1) *passionately* given, and (2) where there are *clear benefits to you* are very persuasive.

The huge problem with referrals

So, what *is* the problem with referrals? They seem so ideal. There can't be any, can there?

Well …

> The huge problem with referrals is … you never get enough of them.

And that's it.

If people recommended you more, there would be no downside to referrals. They're easier to close, quick, there are less objections. It's cheaper than spending money on brochures and adverts. There are *no downsides*. Except that people don't recommend you enough.

When you think about it, to grow your business by referral, you are going to have to rely on *other people* recommending you.

And here's the rub: relying on others to refer you means that you are *delegating the speed of growth of your business to third parties.*

And these third parties will have other things to do that are more important to them than referring you to their contacts. Like, running their own businesses ... getting on with their lives ...

But, imagine if you knew simple ways to proactively trigger referrals – meaning *you* were in charge of the growth of your company, not the third party. In other words, imagine getting all the benefits of referral business – lots of cheap, easy sales – without the only problem with them.

You're about to discover how to do just that ...

GETTING THE 'REFERRAL FOUNDATIONS' RIGHT

Getting the definitions sorted

Just like at school – when (1) you, (2) your friend, and (3) the person of your dreams were all involved in the process of getting you a date – so too does referral business involve three people:

1 you;
2 the person who is going to refer you; and
3 the person you want to speak to.

Or, to use snappier titles:

1 you;
2 referrer; and
3 target.

In other words, you want the referrer to recommend you to your target (Fig. 6.4).

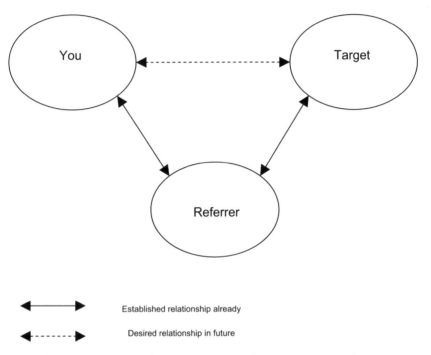

Figure 6.4 'You want the referrer to recommend you to your target.'

The only other thing to define here is my understanding of what a referral is. To my mind, it has four elements:

- a personal recommendation (i.e. by the referrer) …
- … to someone you don't yet know, but want to (your target) …
- … such that your target is expecting your call for business purposes …
- … and is looking forward to it.

If any of these is missing, it's not a referral. This means the referrer *has* to warm the target up before you call them. If they don't, and you ring saying, 'Hi Jill, I'm John. Bob Jones has suggested I call you', this has less chance of success since Jill has not heard of you yet, meaning you still have her initial objections to overcome.

So, now we know the four definitions we need to know – you, referrer, target, referral – let's look at the golden rules of referrals.

The golden rules of referrals
Rule 1: To get referrals, you are going to have to do more than nothing.
The first rule is simple, yet often overlooked.

Remember what you've just read about *you* dictating the speed of growth of your company, and not a third party? This first rule reminds you that getting referrals is an *active* process, rather than you simply waiting for them to happen.

There's a feeling prevalent in business that 'we do a good job; so customers are bound to recommend us', but they usually don't. Sure, some do; but it's much rarer than you would expect.

There are all sorts of reasons for this. For example your customers aren't in the habit of referring you, so don't think about it; they're busy doing other things rather than helping a supplier (i.e. you) get more business, and so on.

But the biggest problem is that customers demand exceptional service these days. Any less and they'll tell people how bad you were. But do a great job, and it's what they were expecting anyway, so why tell anyone?

Reminder of rule 1

To get referrals, you are going to have to do more than nothing.

Rule 2: For the referral to work, there must be an obvious benefit to all three parties.
There are three parties involved in the referral – you, the referrer, and the target.

If one of the three doesn't benefit, it's not a successful, sustainable business process, meaning you are unlikely to get any future referrals involving these two parties again. And, given how we've decided referrals are the best way of marketing, doing something that prevents future referrals is little short of a disaster.

A few years ago, one of my good friends Tom wanted to help his friend, a landscape gardener, get more business. So Tom recommended him to one of his neighbours.

The gardener visited the neighbour, priced up the work, but then submitted an extortionate quote. The neighbour wasn't happy and spoke to Tom, saying that the price was too high and that he wanted to go back and ask for a reduction.

Immediately, this placed Tom in a terrible position. He couldn't see any way out of this which would leave all three parties unscathed.

If Tom said to his neighbour, 'Sure, go for a reduction in price,' the gardener might come back to Tom saying that Tom had recommended him to somebody who wouldn't pay his worth. However, if Tom said 'No, I'm sure the price is fair,' he would damage his relationship with his neighbour. What would you do in this position? It certainly made Tom wish he hadn't tried to help.

In the end, the neighbour respectfully declined the offer from the gardener and gave the job to someone else. Fortunately, all parties stayed on good terms.

But it could have gone disastrously wrong. This is typical of the problems with referrals. They are such a delicate balancing act to make sure that all parties are happy. So, you must make sure *both* the referrer and the target are happy with the work you do, and the way you do it.

> **Reminder of Rule 2**
>
> For the referral to work, there must be an obvious benefit to all three parties.

Rule 3: It is your responsibility – nobody else's – to make it crystal clear to the referrer how both the referrer and the target will benefit from the referral.
The final rule is a combination of rule 1 – you must do something – and rule 2 – all three parties must benefit.

The referrer must be in *no doubt at all* that both they and the target will benefit (remember, the person who is a target for you is a good contact of the referrer).

Table 6.2 shows various ways that people traditionally ask for referrals and whether each of the three parties benefit or not.

Lines people say	Benefit to you?	Benefit to the referrer?	Benefit to the target?
'Do you know anyone I can do business with?'	Yes		
'I help architects. Do you know any?'	Yes		Yes
'You know I've done a good job for you. Do you know anyone else who I could work with?'	Yes		Implied
'I gave you a referral last week. Have you anyone you can refer me to?'	Yes		
'I pay finders fees for introductions.'	Yes	Yes	

Table 6.2 Various ways that people traditionally ask for referrals and whether each of the three parties benefit of not

None of these phrases clearly benefits all three parties, so none is likely to work most of the time. I mean, would you recommend your supplier to someone just because they asked you to, without there being any benefit to you, or to your contact you will be referring them to?

The bottom sentence (about finders fees) is an interesting one, because people often offer finders fees in return for referrals. But this seldom works well on its own. The fact that there's no benefit to the target is part of the reason for this, as is the fact that a small amount of money is not the main motivator for a referrer, as we will see later.

Reminder of the three rules

1 To get referrals, you are going to have to do more than nothing.
2 For the referral to work, there must be an obvious benefit to all three parties.
3 It is your responsibility to make it crystal clear to the referrer how both the referrer and the target will benefit from the referral.

Why everyone benefits from referrals
Rule 2 says that all three parties must benefit from a referral, and rule 3 says it's *your* responsibility to ensure the referrer knows this will happen.

This sounds a big task. How can you persuade a referrer that all three parties are going to benefit from recommending *you* such that *you* get more business? Fortunately, this is much easier than you think:

Benefits to you
These are obvious. More business, easy sales, low cost, less time, no jelly, no hassle, no unpleasantness.

Benefits to target

Put yourself in the target's position. How would *you* rather choose your suppliers:

- from the Yellow Pages;
- scanning the Internet; or
- someone you trust recommending someone *they* trust.

Everyone chooses the last one. Very often, a company's best suppliers started as recommendations from others. They are best, partly because they were good enough to be recommended in the first place, but partly because they don't want to let their referrer down.

You'll have benefited from this yourself. For instance, when you last moved into a new area and wanted a good decorator, cleaner, and the best local restaurant, how did you go about it? No doubt by asking somebody you knew to recommend them.

It's the same in business. If your business needs a new stationery supplier, it's so much easier, better, cheaper and guaranteed to work to ask your business contacts to recommend a good one.

So, yes, targets like referrals. They *seek* referrals. And that brings us on to:

Benefits to referrers

As a child, I used to love it when my relatives gave me money at Christmas. Some of them did it sometimes; some of them – I'm devastated to say – didn't do it very much at all. However, my Auntie Ethel – God rest her soul – always used to bring me money every Christmas without fail. And – though I know this makes me come across as a very shallow child – I therefore used to like Auntie Ethel *best*.

And similarly, since – as we've just seen – targets love referrals, they're going to like *best* the regular bringers of referrals, i.e. referrers.

And, that's just the start of the benefits to referrers. You see, they are the only party with two established relationships here (Fig. 6.5).

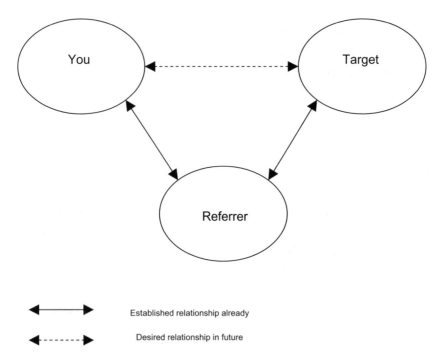

Figure 6.5 The referrer is the only party with two established relationships.

So, a brilliant referral will mean they're positively contributing to *two* people, not one.

And this means twice the benefits to them:

- they'll look good to the *target* – helpful, life-saver, well connected, good person to know, etc.; and
- *you* will be grateful, which means you'll be thanking them in some way (see page 176).

These two effects are made even more pronounced by the fact that there is a lot of research around showing that, for the most part, people are generally *reciprocator,s* i.e. they want to repay kind acts: you help me; I'll help you.

So, a referrer giving to *two* people has a very good chance of their help being reciprocated in some way.

HOW TO GET MORE REFERRALS

So far in this section, you have seen countless advantages of growing your business using referrals. In fact, there is only one problem with referrals: people don't give you enough of them.

It's now time to find out what you need to do and say to proactively trigger as many referrals as possible. There are five steps (Table 6.3):

Step	Title	Details
1	Never underestimate their power	It will take effort for the referrals to start rolling in so always remember how valuable they are – it helps keep you motivated.
2	The pre-prep you must do	The two things you *must know* in advance of asking for referrals.
3	Who to ask for referrals	Certain groups of people are more likely to refer you than others. This step shows who to target first.
4	Jelly-free scripts to use to get referrals	You must ask for referrals in the right way. This section contains scripts you can use.
5	How to ensure you keep getting them	Some simple tips to make sure referrals become a long-term, source of business for you.

Table 6.3 Five steps to getting more referrals

Step 1 – Never underestimate their power

How many people would you say you know well enough to pick up the phone to have a chat with?

Your answer will be surprisingly high. If you were to include family members, friends, customers, staff/colleagues, school friends, business contacts, suppliers, your neighbours, friends from your church, cricket club, etc. ... When you think of all these different sources, it's probably going to be at least a hundred people.

But, to be prudent (as we accountants like to say), let's assume you have fifty people that you can pick up the phone to.

Now, the same question from *their* point of view. How many good friends/contacts do *your contacts* have? Again, let's go with an average of fifty each.

So, from a potential referral point of view, you could – in theory – ring each of your fifty friends and ask them to recommend you to their fifty friends.

Fifty people making fifty calls each is 2500 calls. This means that you are only two phone calls away from 2500 people (Fig 6.6) – and both

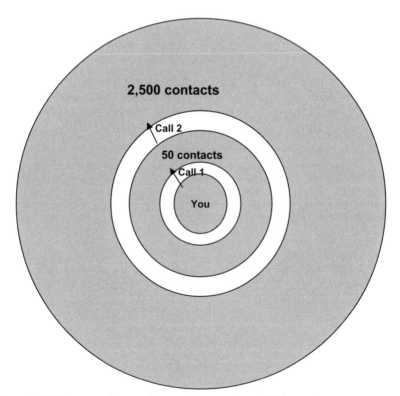

Figure 6.6 'You are only two phone calls away from 2500 people.'

of these phone calls would have been made between two sets of good friends (you and the referrer, and the referrer and the target).

There is a very good chance that some of these 2500 people would need your services. This means that, with the right scripts, you could be speaking to lots of warmed up referrals about ten minutes from now.

So, the power of referrals is enormous. Remember that at all times in your business ... it will help you focus on getting more of them.

Step 2 – Pre-prep you must do
Recommending a DVD
There are only two things to prepare in advance to get lots of referrals. The first is best displayed by the following exercise:

I want to buy a DVD for someone I love very much. I would like you to think of *any* DVD I could give them. Write the first one that pops into your head here:

I am now going to give you a bit more information about the person I love. If – after hearing this information – you want to amend your choice of DVD, simply write a new title in the box below.

The person is female ...

Does your suggested DVD change if I tell you that this person is my daughter Megan, who is nine years old ...

There are many types of films that Megan likes, but she's always loved films with animals in. What DVD would you suggest now?

```



```

One thing I've also noticed is that she prefers live-action films to cartoons. So, she wouldn't want a DVD of an animated film. So, what DVD now?

```



```

Finally, one thing I should have told you before is that her favourite film of all time is 'Lassie', and she hasn't got it on DVD. What DVD do you advise I buy her?

```



```

Lassie, right?

This exercise highlights a paradox with referrals. From *my* point of view, I thought I was helping you when I asked you to recommend *any* DVD, because it gave you lots of options. But, actually, I didn't give you enough direction. So, you initially recommended a DVD she wouldn't like. It was only when I became more precise that it became easy for you to recommend something useful to me.

And that is *exactly* the same with asking for referrals. If you say to the referrer that you want to speak to '*any*body who needs my services', it is very hard for them to know who to target for you. It's too vague.

So, the first thing to prepare is:

Required information 1: who do you want to speak to?

Remember, golden rule 2 of referrals is *all three parties* must benefit. The referrer doesn't benefit much if they have to spend ages working out who to refer you to.

You already know the answer to 'Who do you want to speak to?': the big fish you identified in the Networking section (page 27 onwards). You want referrals into these industries.

Quick reminder

Big fish are the professions which:

* give you the most income, and/or
* give you the most enjoyment, and/or
* you have the biggest potential to help.

Required information 2: the AFTERs for each of your big fish

The only other information you need is what each of your big fish are left with AFTER you have worked with them (re-read page 9 for a reminder of the AFTERs).

Let's say you are a photographer, and a big fish for you is a graphic designer who can use your photographs in the brochures they design.

The AFTERs *for them* – the graphic designer – might include:

* Their brochures will look better because of the quality of photographs you produce.
* They will therefore impress their clients more.
* They will have an improved portfolio to show to potential new customers.

- They will have greater pride in the work they do.
- Because of your unique style, they will be able to offer their customers something that other graphic designers can't.
- Your reliability means that they will always meet their deadlines.

To get maximum use out of the rest of this section, it's worth preparing this information now, before reading on. Insert your big fish in the left hand column of Table 6.4, and the AFTERs you leave *them* with on the right …

Big Fish (Profession)	AFTERs (*they* are left with)

Table 6.4 The AFTERs you leave your big fish with

Now you have this information, the only things you need to know are:

- who to ask for referrals;
- jelly-free scripts; and
- how to ensure you keep getting referrals in the long term.

Looking at each in turn:

Step 3 – Who to ask for referrals

In Ivan Misner's book *Business by Referral* he lists various types of potential referrers. These include:

Your customers

Customers can always refer you by telling others of the work you've done for them.

After all, if you've done good work for customer A, you are surely in a good bargaining position for them to introduce you to customer B and customer C.

So customers can be a great source of referrals. But there are others …

Your friends and family

There is a very prominent local radio presenter, in my home city of Liverpool. When I first started in business I wanted to meet him.

So I asked Jane, a woman who was doing my PR for me, to get me a meeting with this man. Jane used her connections well; it took a while but she somehow managed to arrange it.

I was delighted, and spoke to my parents about how much I was looking forward to meeting him, and how pleased I was with all the hard work that Jane had put in …

To which Mum replied, 'Oh, I know him. We work on a committee together with a local charity. I've got his number in my mobile phone.'

Unbelievable! Jane had spent *weeks* making this appointment, and my mother could have done it for me straight away.

But then it got worse … my father chipped in with, 'Actually Andy, I know him very well too.'

So, *both* my parents knew him extremely well. But, when I asked – in a rather exasperated tone – 'Why didn't you introduce him to me?', they replied …

'Because you didn't ask.'

This is typical. Your friends and family know so many people. They are *bound* to know someone you want to speak to.

I know many people like to separate their business and personal lives. And, if you are like this, it's probably best you don't ask friends and family for referrals. However, although it can feel strange to discuss referrals with them, there is probably no-one more motivated to help you.

Your suppliers

Suppliers are a hugely under-utilized source of referrals. When you think about it, you have no power whatsoever over your customers (after all, 'the customer is always right') … yet people still ask them for referrals.

But, when speaking to your suppliers, *you* are the customer. So, *you* are always right. Why not ask them for referrals? If anything, they will be keener to help you than anybody, to preserve the good trading relations between you.

When I tell my clients about asking suppliers, very often they reply, 'That doesn't feel right'. But, when I ask, 'Why not?', the only thing they come back with is, 'Because we've never tried it before.'

I said elsewhere that, as customers, we want our suppliers to be *problem solvers* not technicians. So, a supplier who can get you referred business becomes a great *problem solver* – they solve you the problem of finding customers yourself!

Tennis teams

It's great fun watching tennis, especially if you are sitting level with the net and see the ball being bashed from side to side.

By 'tennis team referrals', I mean referral partners, whereby you and they regularly pass work to each other, just like tennis players hitting the ball to each other.

For instance, one of the things I do is teach companies to sell more. Therefore, if I work closely with a marketing company, we can regularly pass work to each other. I can say to my clients:

> *'I can help you close more sales when you're in front of people. But, wouldn't it be great if you were actually in front of more people? Well, I know this great marketing company who are experts at helping you do this.'*

Similarly, the marketing company could say to all their clients:

> *'All the work we've done will get you in front of your target market more than ever. However, unless you say the right things when you're there, you are not going to get the sales you want, so you're not going to get the maximum return on your investment with us. We know this guy called Andy Bounds who will show you how to turn these new meetings into sales.'*

So, which professions could you play referral tennis with?

Staff

Earlier, you saw how *everyone* has at least fifty people they could pick the phone up to at any time.

Your staff are the same. In fact, knowing the way these things work, I would expect that many organizations are missing lots of excellent referrals just because they've not asked their staff.

Instead, they will be using all the traditional marketing tools – direct mail, advertising, PR, networking, cold calling, blanket mail-drops … *everything.* Except, of course, asking Sally in the post room – whose father happens to be the CEO of their number 1 target company.

People who you have given referrals to in the past

I mentioned earlier how most people are reciprocators.

So, if you have given a referral to someone in the past, there is a very good chance they'll reciprocate by finding you a referral.

People who have given you referrals in the past

It's always nerve-racking referring someone for the first time. How good a job will they do? Will your contact like them?

After the first referral's proved successful, it's relatively easy to give more. So, people who've referred you in the past are excellent sources of new referrals.

Step 4 – Jelly-free scripts that get referrals

Before looking at what to say to get referrals, it's worth a quick reminder of the three golden rules in Table 6.5 to see if we are obeying them so far:

Rule	How are we doing so far?
1 You must do more than nothing.	Yes, because we are doing something to get more referrals right now!
2 For referrals to work, there must be an obvious benefit to all three parties.	Your target will benefit, by receiving the AFTERs you highlighted in the table on page 158. Your referrers will benefit because they: • have helped you get more business; • have helped the target (through you) achieve the AFTERs mentioned above; • look good to both you and the target (because they have helped you both).
3 It is your responsibility to make it crystal clear to the referrer how both the referrer and the target will benefit from the referral.	To do this, you need to say the right thing when asking for a referral. This section will give you scripts to use to make the benefits to everybody crystal clear.

Table 6.5 A quick reminder of the three golden rules and how we're doing so far

Whatever scripts you use to get referrals must give clear guidance so the referrer knows *exactly* who you want to speak to. It is no use saying, 'Do you know *any*body?' (That's like saying 'recommend *any* DVD'.) Your table on page 158 is going to be critical to achieving this.

Your customers

Since all the parties must benefit, simply saying, 'Can you recommend me to anyone?' isn't sufficient. You look like you are lining your pocket with little or no thought for the referrer or target. These three scripts work much better:

Script 1

'Have you found the work we have done useful?' [Yes.]

'Do you know anyone else I could similarly help? From experience, I know I have the biggest impact with [mention two or three big fish from your table], because I can help with their [list the AFTERs you produce for these big fish].'

[If they say 'Yes, I know someone.']

'Brilliant, thank you. How can I best help you make this happen?' [Then, do whatever they ask of you, to make the introduction *easy for them*.]

This script works. Firstly, it is clear to the referrer that both they and the target are going to benefit from the referral. Your first sentence reinforces how helpful you have been to the referrer, and they can easily deduce how helpful you will be to their contacts (your target).

Your second sentence gets rid of the 'DVD problem' because you have been specific in who you want to speak to, and how they will benefit from speaking to you.

Assuming they know someone they could refer you to, the third sentence is a great way to show them that you are going to proactively help make it happen.

Here's a second script that works very well:

Script 2

'Have you found the work we did helpful?' [Yes.]

'That's great news. The reason I can provide these high levels of service is because I spend 95% of my time looking after my existing customers, like you; and only 5% of my time looking for new clients.

'The reason I am able to spend only 5% of my time looking for new business is because I grow my business by word of mouth.

'I get my best results with [big fish], by helping them [AFTERs]. Do you know any of these professions you could introduce me to please?' [Yes.]

'How can I best help you make this happen?'

The inference here is that the reason your customer has just bene-fited from your outstanding work is because previous customers – i.e. *people like them* – have helped you get more business, thus freeing up your time for their benefit.

Customers hearing this often want to join in and introduce you to people *they* know, because that keeps your time free to focus on your customers, like themselves.

Again, the third golden rule is adhered to here, since it's clear to the referrer how everyone will benefit by passing your name on.

A third script you can use is what I call the 'Ask you later' method. There are two phases to this script. You say the first *as the customer is signing up, i.e. before you have done any work.*

Script 3 – phase 1

'Thank you for choosing us. We are really looking forward to working with you.

'Just so you know, the way we work is this: once we have finished a particular project with a customer, and we have ensured they are absolutely delighted with everything we have done, we always ask them to recommend us to their contacts for whom we could provide a similarly excellent service.

'Are you okay with us discussing this after our work together?'

Taken out of context, this script can appear over the top.

But it only takes 10–20 seconds, and happens at the end of a very productive meeting. (The meeting obviously went well or they would not just have bought from you.) So, it is easy for them to reply, 'Sure, no problem', and then forget all about it.

Then, of course comes your work with them and you have to pull out all the stops, and do a great job.

Once you have finished – and impressed and delighted them – you then do the second part of the script:

> **Script 3 – phase 2**
>
> 'So, are you happy with how everything has gone?' [Yes.]
>
> 'Great. So are we.
>
> 'Do you remember, when we first agreed to work together, I said that – after the successful completion of this project – I would ask if you would be happy to refer me to your contacts?' [They will either remember (which they probably will), or you might need to remind them.]
>
> 'Well, the professions where I do my best work is [big fish], because I help them [AFTERs]. Who do you know who works in these professions?'
>
> [And, if they know someone …]
>
> 'How can I best help you make this happen?'

When the customer originally said they'd help you if you did a great job, the two of you made a very informal verbal contract. You have done your bit – you did a great job – now you are asking them to do theirs.

Hopefully, they'll know a big fish, and you've got yourself another referral.

If however it turns out they don't know anyone they can refer you to, or they decide they don't want to, that's no problem. It's a shame, but no relations have been soured between you, because they had previously agreed that you could ask them.

Again, note the last sentence in the box – 'How can I best help you make this happen?' It comes up time and again in the scripts in this chapter. Once your contact has agreed to help you get a referral, proactively help them do it.

> **Simple summary of referral scripts for your customers:**
>
> 1 'Have you found the work useful?' [Yes.] 'Well, please can you ...'
> 2 'I spend 95% of my time looking after my clients ...'
> 3 The two-part 'Ask you later' method.

Your friends and family

You will know your relationship with your friends and family better than I ever could, so I wouldn't presume to give you the scripts to use with them.

Instead, all I would ask you to remember is the reason my parents gave for not introducing me to that radio presenter:

'You never asked'.

The simplest thing to do is to show your friends/family your big fish/AFTERs table and say to them, 'Do you know any of these?' (pointing to the left hand column), 'because I can help them do that' (pointing to the right).

If they say 'yes', simply ask – *as you always must* – 'How can I best help you make this happen?'

> **Simple summary of referral scripts for your friends and family**
>
> 1 If you don't ask, you don't get. Show them your big fish/AFTERs table and ask if they know anyone.
> 2 'How can I best help you make this happen?'

Your suppliers

From your suppliers' point of view – *you* are the *customer*. Therefore, feel free simply to ask them for referrals.

Script for suppliers

'Thanks for all the great work that you do. There's another way that you can help us which we haven't spoken about yet.' ['What's that?']

'Well, we grow our business by word of mouth. We ask people to recommend us to our target market. Would you be happy doing this for us?' [They will say yes. They want to help you. You're their customer!]

'Great,' … big fish/AFTERs … 'How can I best help you make this happen?'

That's it. Very easy. Simply ask the question, and you'll get a surprisingly high success rate.

If you don't ask, they probably won't think of doing it, since they don't see their role as helping your sales go up.

And, it's not just with *existing* suppliers that this works. Try this with *potential new* suppliers …

Script for potential new suppliers

'The sales pitch you have shown us was very impressive, and no doubt you will be able to help our business. But, there is one other thing we look for before taking on new suppliers. We grow our business by word of mouth, so ask our suppliers to refer us into people they know. Would you be happy to help us get more business in?' [Yes.]

'Great,'…big fish/AFTERs … 'How can I best help you make this happen?'

Again, very simple, and very effective. After all, if it was *you* who was tendering for work, and your potential customer asked you if you could refer them into your contacts, you'd try and help. After all, it might help you get the sale.

Simple summary of referral scripts for your suppliers

Existing suppliers – Thank them for what they do, then ask them.

Potential suppliers – Remember to ask them. They are keen to help you.

Tennis teams

Referral tennis teams are when professions work closely with each other, passing regular work each way. For example, estate agents and mortgage advisors; accountants and solicitors; graphic designers and printers, etc.

The script to use here is one that makes it clear from the outset that you are looking for a long-term referral relationship. Something like:

Script for tennis partners

'What we do is so compatible that I really think we can both help each other's business grow. Do you?' [Yes.]

'The way I suggest we do this is you tell me the types of profession you want to work with, and I will see who I can introduce you to. Would that be okay?' [Of course!]

'And then, I can show you my [big fish/AFTERs], and you can similarly help me. Would that be okay?' [Of course!]

'When I am looking for referrals for you, it will really help me if you can advise me on the things to say to give you the best chance of getting these referrals. Would you be happy to do this?' [Of course!]

'And, if you don't mind, can I give you similar scripts so you have the best chance of getting referrals for me?' [Of course!]

Your initial sentence showed that *both* parties would benefit, and made clear to your tennis partner that you weren't looking just to line your own pocket.

You then showed them that you wanted to help *their* business *first*. It's very easy when talking to a potential referrer to go straight for the kill for *your* business. However, since people reciprocate, you might as well offer to help them first.

The two sentences at the bottom ensure that you will be specific with each other's big fish/AFTERs, rather than leaving it with, 'Do you know *anybody* you can introduce me to?'

> **Simple summary for referral scripts for your tennis partners ...**
>
> 1 You want a long-term relationship.
> 2 So, offer to help them first.
> 3 Be specific with your big fish, to help each other.

Your staff

There are two problems with asking staff for referrals:

- they don't see it as their job; and
- often they don't want to discuss your company with their personal friends.

Whatever script you use must be mindful of these two points, and must never make them feel awkward or compromised.

There are various ways you can ask them, but the simplest and least invasive is to simply put your big fish/AFTERs table on a wall in the office, and let everyone know that:

- these are good contacts for your company;
- it is a huge contribution to the company for any staff member to recommend you to any big fish they know; and
- they will be rewarded in some way if they do.

This is the least risky way of doing it. You won't get as many referrals as if you went to each member of staff individually and said, 'Do you know any of these companies?', but nor will you place any of your staff in an awkward situation, whereby they feel they have to do something outside work that they don't want to do.

Of course, if a member of staff *does* provide a referral for you, then it is important to give them the appropriate recognition, since recognition is one of the greatest motivators there is. Imagine how many referrals your staff would get if you always publicly recognized them in a way that made them feel special.

Simple summary of referral scripts for your staff

1 Don't pressurize them.
2 Let them know your big fish/AFTERs.
3 Make it clear that referral-givers will be rewarded.
4 Publicly recognize those staff who get referrals.

People who you have given referrals to in the past

People who have previously received referrals from you will be motivated to help you in return, making the script fairly simple:

Script for past receivers of referrals

'Did you find that referral I gave you helpful?' [Yes.]

'I was wondering, could you help me in a similar way? Do you know anybody to whom you could refer me?' [Yes.]

'Great,' … big fish/AFTERs … 'How can I best help you make this happen?'

That's all you need to do. It is important you first remind them that you've already helped them – since it puts their 'debt' to you in the forefront of their mind – *before* you ask for help.

There are alternatives to all these scripts, of course. For instance, one of my clients – a bank manager – uses a tennis analogy when asking for referrals from someone to whom he has referred work in the past. He simply says, 'That's 15–love to me. Your serve.'

His approach works for him. My approach works for me. What's the best approach for you? As ever, the answer to that question is: 'Whichever *works*'.

Simple summary of referral scripts for past receivers of referrals

1 Remind them you helped them.
2 Ask for a referral.

People who have given you referrals in the past

Script for people who have given you referrals in the past

'Thanks for that referral you gave me the other day. It went really well. What happened was … [tell the story].'

'While I was working with him, I was really mindful of making sure I did a good job for *you* because you had referred me in. Are you happy with how everything went?' [Yes.]

'Great. Because everything worked so well last time, it got me thinking … do you know anyone else who I could similarly help? The people I tend to work with are [big fish/AFTERs].' [Yes.]

'How can I best help you make this happen?'

Once they have said that you did a good job (in effect, you made them look good in the target's eyes), *then* is the time to ask for another referral. Again, you will note that you are using the same lines as usual – big fish/AFTERs/ 'How can I best help you make this happen?'

> **Simple summary of referral scripts for people who have given you referrals in the past**
>
> 1 Thank them for the referral again.
> 2 Ensure they were happy with how you did.
> 3 Ask them for another ...

Step 5 – Ensuring you get referrals in the long term

You have now done four of the five steps. To remind yourself of them, look at Table 6.6:

Step	Title
1	Never underestimate their power
2	Pre-prep you must do
3	Who to ask for referrals
4	Jelly-free scripts to use to get them

Table 6.6 The first four of the five steps needed to get referrals in the long term

These four steps – though good – will only give you referrals in the *short term*.

And, since we have decided that referrals are the best way to market your business, you want referrals to be a sustainable, long-term source of sales.

Since giving you referrals can be nerve-racking the first time, it is easier to get *two referrals from one person*, than one referral each from two different people.

So, you must do everything in your power to make people give you *as many referrals as possible*. Here are some simple techniques to help you do that:

Continual feedback

If you give me a referral into one of your valued contacts, you will want to know how things are going throughout my dealings with her.

So I need to let you know the outcome of every interaction I have, including:

- the first call;
- our meeting(s) together;
- the date any work is going to start;
- how the work is progressing; and
- what she said at the end of the work.

This is the *minimum* I must do. Any less and you might think that you have become unimportant to me, compared with my growing relationship with the target (your contact).

Rewarding the referrer

Imagine you received three things today: a gift-wrapped present, a new piece of work from an existing customer and a referral. Who would you give most thanks to – the present-giver, the existing customer or the referrer?

Most people, if answering truthfully, would say their most gushing thanks would be reserved for the present-giver. You might give them a hug, buy them something in return, etc.

But, for some reason, on receiving a *referral*, referrers often don't get the thanks they deserve. Certainly, not as gushing as if they had simply bought you a present ... which may be of negligible value compared with a referred piece of work.

To thank them you could simply say 'thank you', or you might like to buy them something – a gift, a handwritten card, offer your business services to them for free, take them out for a meal, publicize their business to your contacts … *anything*.

However, the one thing you must avoid is … doing nothing.

Ivan Misner, BNI's founder, says the best mechanism for rewarding people who give you referrals is a mechanism you won't ever forget doing. He says that if you dislike writing, there is no point thinking you will send handwritten cards all the time, because it's not in your nature to do so.

So, decide on how you want to thank/reward your referrers, and stick to it.

Who helps who first?

There are two ways you can get referrals from your referrers. Either, get referrals off them first, and then give them some back. Or, you give to them first, such that they want to help you in return.

Which is the better option? I have mentioned BNI and Ivan Misner a great deal in this chapter because this chapter is about *referrals* and BNI is the largest *referral* organisation in the world. Their motto is 'Givers gain' – the more you give to others, the more you gain because they give back to you. And if it is the ethos by which the largest referral organization in the world lives its life, it's a pretty good motto for us all to take on board if we want to get more referrals from our business contacts.

Presentations

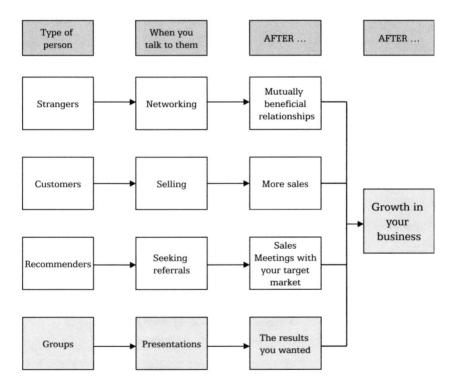

Type of person	When you talk to them	AFTER ...	AFTER ...
Strangers	Networking	Mutually beneficial relationships	
Customers	Selling	More sales	Growth in your business
Recommenders	Seeking referrals	Sales Meetings with your target market	
Groups	Presentations	The results you wanted	

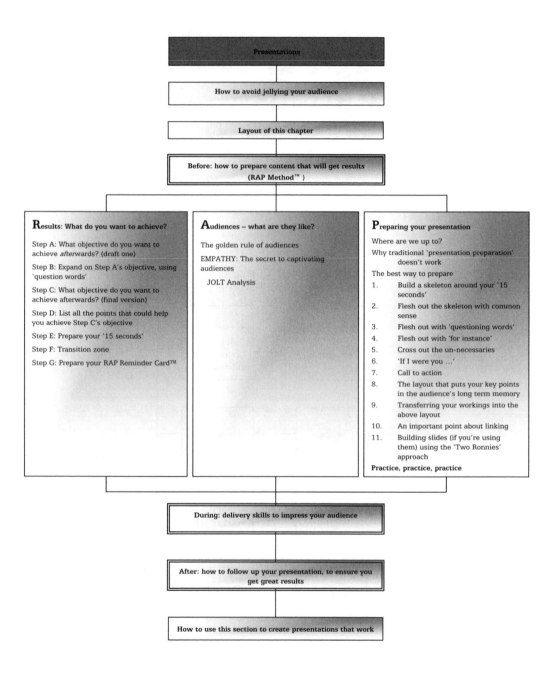

HOW TO AVOID JELLYING YOUR AUDIENCE

How many times have you been speaking in front of a group and been unsure about what's about to come out of your mouth?

But, it's not only your mind that can go. There are *so many things* to focus on. Your body language, your content, what the slides should look like. What to wear, what to do with your hands, how to phrase your key points. What to do with your voice, how to present with charisma, how to create an aura as you speak. How to get buy-in from your audience, how to engage them, handling your nerves, the best way to practise. The list goes on and on …

In my job, I coach people how to do all these things. But for the purpose of this book, I'm going to focus on just one aspect: reducing your jelly. In other words, getting your content *exactly right*, so that you:

- engage your audience; and
- have the best chance of achieving your desired results from your presentation.

These aren't easy skills to master. But learn and apply the content of this chapter, and you will be streets ahead of 99% of the presenters out there.

Hard to believe? Well, how many times have you sat through a presentation and been bored, or found the content irrelevant, or thought the presenter was waffling? How many times have you been reading the slides instead of listening to the presenter? How many times have you realized the slides were really prompts for the presenter, rather than being designed to make your audience experience better? How many times have you not even understood what the presenter was talking about?

And the biggest presenter crime of all ... how many times have you sat through a presentation and not known what you are supposed to do at the end, after hearing it?

You see, presentations are often full of irrelevant jelly.

They are not audience-focussed.

To be blunt, they can be utterly boring.

In this section, you will discover how to prepare jelly-free, engaging presentations that get great results. I'll cover the three critical elements to making presentations successful – the before, during and after. Or, to give them proper titles:

- *Before*: how to prepare content that gets results (RAP Method™);
- *During*: delivery skills to impress your audiences; and
- *After*: how to follow up your presentations, to ensure they work.

LAYOUT OF THIS CHAPTER

In my experience, people find it easiest to learn what I'm about to share with you through a mixture of:

- hearing the rules; and
- seeing them applied to a worked example.

So, this chapter follows a different format from the rest of the book. Here, you will read the rules of successful presenting, with each rule being followed by a worked example that develops through the chapter.

Before – how to prepare content that will get results (RAP Method™)

How do *you* prepare for presentations?

- In an absolute blind panic … you've not left enough time to prepare properly – again.
- Use last time's presentation, with the minimum possible changes (preparing this way is often accompanied by this conversation with a colleague: 'But last time's didn't work' … 'I know, but this time it just might').
- Start by writing your PowerPoint slides, and then – once they're finished – thinking, 'Now, what do I want to say?'

Recognise any/all of these? Unfortunately, none is efficient or logical.

When you think about it, the key to getting positive *results* from a presentation is to first know what *results* you want to achieve. So, you need to start your preparation by thinking of this first.

But you won't achieve these *results* unless your audience does what you want after hearing you. So, you need to consider them next.

And only after you've thought through both these areas – your results and the audience – can you start preparing your presentation.

So, the process for preparing successful presentations – *and I strongly advise you to use this every single time* – is a three-step process I've developed: my RAP Method™:

Results – what do you want to achieve?

Audience – what are they like?

Preparation – only do this once you've addressed the first two areas.

Results: What do you want to achieve?

There are seven steps to establishing your results:

A   What objective do you want to achieve *after*wards (draft one)?
B   Expand on step A's objective, using 'question words'.
C   What objective do you want to achieve *after*wards (final version)?
D   List all the points that could help you achieve step C's objective.
E   Prepare your '15 seconds'.
F   Transition zone.
G   Prepare your RAP Reminder Card™.

Step A – What objective do you want to achieve afterwards? (draft one)

If you take only one thing from this section, let it be this:

> For you to achieve a great *result* from your presentation, the first thing you must know is the *result* you want to achieve.

To find this, ask yourself: 'What do I want my audience to do after hearing me speak? How will *I* judge if this presentation has been a success?'

Example

Imagine you run a department of a large accountancy practice. You're in charge of ensuring that this department meets their sales targets. You've identified that your department is currently very poor at networking – your staff rarely attend events and, when they do, it never leads to business.

You want to make a presentation to your staff about networking. So, before putting pen to paper, you need to decide what you're seeking to achieve. It could simply be:

'I want them to go networking.'

Step B – Expand on step A's objective, using questioning words
The next step makes sure that step A's objective is right, and that you haven't missed anything out.

The best way to do this is to ask yourself questions about the objective you wrote in step A, by using all of the questioning words – why, when, who, where, how, etc. – to draw more points out.

Example

Objective: 'I want them to go networking.'
Why?

- To increase our sales.
- To build the profile of the business.
- To increase their skills.
- To increase the selling mentality of the department.

When?

- Start now.
- Then, ongoing.

Who?

- My eight customer-facing staff, plus their two managers.

Where?

- Chamber of Commerce.
- BNI.
- Institute of Directors.

How?

- Not relevant here – I'll teach them networking skills later.
- I just want their buy-in for now.
- Crucially, I want them to *want to* go and network.

Step C – What objective do you want to achieve afterwards? (final version)

You can now create the official version of your objective by enhancing your draft one objective (step A) with the answers to step B's questions. This will lead to a long sentence, covering *everything* you want to achieve.

Example

'I want to increase our department's sales, by getting all my customer-facing staff to *want* to go networking at Chamber of Commerce, BNI and the Institute of Directors, from now onwards.'

Step D– List all the points that could help you achieve step C's objective

This step is something presenters rarely do at this stage, if at all. And that is to find *all the points* that give you the greatest chance of achieving your objective.

Traditionally, you see, people start preparing presentations by thinking, 'What should I say on slide 1, then slide 2 …?'

However, that leads to too much jelly, because people often start presentations the same way they started their last one … often, with their date of incorporation!

So, rather than thinking how the presentation should start, you should first identify all the points that give you the best chance of success.

Points to get across

- Our sales will increase.
- We can match our competitors, who are currently attending these events.
- It's what good firms do.
- It creates a buzz in our department.
- It gets my staff out of the office.
- It helps develop us all.
- We can find out what's going on in the city.
- We will meet good suppliers/associates.
- We will hear of big contracts we could pitch for.
- It is a quicker way to get new business than using advertising and PR.
- It's good team-bonding for our group.
- Networking can be fun.
- It's much better than cold calling.

Step E – Prepare your 15 seconds

Imagine you have a presentation to do. It's to an important audience. You want to do a great job. They have graciously given you 30 minutes and you have prepared a truly fantastic presentation. You know it will knock their socks off. Then, just as you open your mouth to speak, you hear the dreaded news …

'I'm sorry, we haven't much time to see you today. You've just got 15 seconds. What did you want to tell us?'

Okay, this isn't very likely to happen. But you must always know your answer to this question, or you won't have the clarity you need on what your key points are.

You'll have listed 10–15 points in step D, but which are the main 3 or 4 you simply *must* get across if you are to achieve your objective? These points will be your 15 seconds.

Remember, you're thinking from your *audience's* point of view here, not yours. So you're looking for the points *they'll* find most compelling.

The best – and easiest – way to establish your 15 seconds is to play *Winner Stays On* with your list in step D. Compare the top two points. Ask yourself which of these points is the most likely to help you achieve step C's objective.

This is the *winner*. It *stays on*. Then, work your way down the list. So, if point 1 is better than point 2, cross point 2 out. Then, compare points 1 and 3. If point 1 is still the *winner*, cross point 3 out, and compare points 1 and 4.

As you do this, you will find there are three or four points that are so fundamentally critical that they simply cannot be crossed out ... and it is *these* that form your 15 seconds.

Example

You know that your team are very much into personal development, but they absolutely despise – with a *passion* – cold calling.

Therefore, their 15 seconds – the points that are most likely to persuade them to want to go networking – are:

- Our sales will increase;
- it helps develop us all; and
- it's much better than cold calling.

Step F – Transition Zone

You need your *audience* to buy into what you're saying; so you must phrase things from *their* point of view, not *yours*, by:

1   writing down your presenter-focussed phrases;
2   thinking what the business AFTERs are for these phrases;
3   thinking what the emotional AFTERs are;
4   improving all these AFTERs using the phrase 'Well that's a good thing for you because', to make sure the benefits *to the audience* are spelt out;
5   circling the most convincing new phrases;
6   creating your audience-focussed phrases from these circled words; and
7   preparing the title for your presentation, using the most persuasive two or three phrases from the above six stages.

At first glance, these seven stages seem extremely confusing. The example beginning opposite will make it much clearer. Read it in conjunction with the seven stages above. (You'll see that the left hand column relates to stage 1, the second column to stage 2 and so on. Stage 7 is on page 192...)

Example

Presenter-focussed phrase	Business AFTER	Emotional AFTER	Well that's a good thing for you because	Audience-focussed phrase
(stage 1)	(stage 2)	(stage 3)	(stage 4)	(stage 6)
Our sales will increase	Sales will increase	You'll feel good	✳ (Your commission will go up)	Your commission will go up through increased sales
It helps develop us all	Business growth / Staff retention / ✳ (Greater promotion opportunities)	A buzz around the office / You feel good because you're developing	You enjoy your job more / More enrichment / Greater pride in your work / ✳ (You'll like it more)	Greater promotion opportunities following the development of new skills
✳ (It's much better than cold calling)	It's a quicker way to build business relationships	Staff will be happier / Less abuse from unhappy cold-call victims		You'll prefer it to cold calling

Key: = ✳ Stage 5

Stage 7

Of the four circles, the two points your staff will like best are:

1 they can earn more commission; and
2 it doesn't involve any cold calling.

Therefore, your presentation's *title* should reflect both these points. After all, calling your presentation 'Networking' doesn't engage them. But this might ...

> 'A new way to earn a lot more commission ... and it's better than cold calling!'

This will appeal to your staff, because it contains their two biggest motivators.

Also, note how the word *new* makes the title more attractive – they'll wonder what the *new* thing is.

The big learning point here:

	You originally thought ...	You now know ...
Title	'Networking'	'A new way to earn a lot more commission ... and it's better than cold calling!'
15 seconds	• Our sales will increase	• Your commission will go up through increased sales
	• It helps develop us all	• Greater promotion opportunities following the development of new skills
	• It's much better than cold calling	• You'll prefer it to cold calling

- In some ways, it's the same presentation.
- But, it's also completely different.
- The content is now audience-focussed.
- They now want to hear what you're about to say.
- And this means they are more likely to buy into the content.
- Which, in turn, means you're more likely to achieve step C's objective.

Step G – Prepare your RAP Reminder Card^{TM}

Steps A to F have provided a robust, audience-focussed skeleton around which to build your presentation.

Once you are used to doing this, you'll find it doesn't take very long at all: 10–15 minutes at most. But this time is critical if your presentation is to work.

The only remaining danger is that – as you get into the detailed preparation – you might go off at a tangent, forgetting all the excellent work you've done.

Avoid this by creating a RAP Reminder Card™ (Table 7.1).

'I want to increase our department's sales, by getting all my customer-facing staff to want to go Networking at Chamber of Commerce, BNI and the Institute of Directors, from now onwards.'	'A new way to earn a lot more commission … and it's better than cold calling!' • Your commission will go up through increased sales. • Greater promotion opportunities following the development of new skills. • You'll prefer it to cold calling.

Table 7.1 Example of a RAP Reminder Card™

- Get a long piece of card.
- Fold it lengthways.
- Lay it on its side (so it's wide but not high).
- On the left hand side, write the final version of your objective (step C).
- On the right hand side, put the title of your talk at the top, and your 15 seconds underneath (all from step F).
- Then, put this card on your desk, next to where you are working. Keep referring to it *throughout your preparation*. It will keep you focussed on what you are trying to achieve, and what the main points are.

Audiences – what are they like?

The golden rule of audiences

Let's face it, your audience isn't 100% focussed on you. They have thousands of things going on inside their heads, like their business, their children, the holiday they have to book, what they're having for tea ...

But you need your audience to be glad they heard your presentation so that they are likely to do what you want them to.

Which leads to the *golden rule of audiences*:

After hearing your presentation, you want your audience to think, 'I'm really glad I heard that'.

Unfortunately, traditional presentations are miles away from achieving this. Standard presentation jelly – like the presenter's year of incorporation, number of offices, etc. – will *never* have the audience thinking, 'I'm really glad I heard that'.

So, how *do you* ensure your audiences are always thinking, 'I'm really glad I heard that'? It's all to do with one simple seven letter word ...

EMPATHY: the secret to captivating audiences

Empathy is defined as 'the ability to identify with and understand another person's feelings or difficulties'.

More simply, it is putting yourself in the audience's shoes, seeing things from their point of view. And the better you do this, the better your chances of saying things they want to act on.

But empathizing is hard to do. It's subjective. If I were to say to you, 'Think of your audience at your next presentation ... and *empathize* with them,' it's not exactly easy to do, is it?

JOLT analysis

A way I developed to empathize with audiences is to JOLT them:

Judged-by

Objectives

Like doing

Time

Judged-by asks, the question, 'How are the audience judged? How do their superiors judge if they have done a good job or not?' Generally, in business, people default to seeking to do well in the areas where they are *judged*. So, since sales people are judged on their sales, most of what they do is geared to increasing their sales figures.

Objectives simply means their business and personal goals. What are they looking to achieve?

Like doing covers what they do in their spare time.

Time focuses on how much/little time they have. The reason this is so important is that if your audience is short of time (and, let's face it, everybody seems to be these days), time is often their overriding priority when deciding how to act.

So, to empathize with your next audience, JOLT them. Think how they're *judged*, what *objectives* they are looking to achieve, what they *like doing*, and what their *time* constraints are. Doing this helps you speak on their level much more.

As to the question of how much JOLTing you should do … if you're doing a key presentation to a smallish group, JOLT everyone individually; if it is for any other presentation, simply JOLT them as a group, which I've done for our worked example overleaf:

Example

JOLT analysis

Judged-by

- sales going up;
- client satisfaction; and
- new contacts made.

Objectives

- promotion as fast as possible;
- more pay;
- to be developed/trained;
- to enjoy their job; and
- to do better than their peers.

Like doing

- chatting;
- making friends;
- challenges; and
- having their curiosity spiked.

Time

- very time-poor.

Preparing your presentation
Where are we up to?
The work you have done so far has led to the creation of two documents:

- a RAP Reminder Card™ (Table 7.2), and
- a JOLT analysis.

'I want to increase our department's sales, by getting all my customer-facing staff to want to go Networking at Chamber of Commerce, BNI and the Institute of Directors, from now onwards.'	'A new way to earn a lot more commission … and it's better than cold calling!' • Your commission will go up through increased sales. • Greater promotion opportunities following the development of new skills. • You'll prefer it to cold calling.

Table 7.2 The RAP Reminder Card™ example from earlier

JOLT analysis

Judged-by

• sales going up;
• client satisfaction; and
• new contacts made

Objectives

• promotion as fast as possible;
• more pay;
• to be developed/trained;
• to enjoy their job; and
• to do better than their peers.

Like doing

• chatting;
• making friends;
• challenges; and
• having their curiosity spiked.

Time

• very time poor.

And, now that you have crystal clear clarity as to:

- what you are trying to achieve, and
- who your audience are,

you can now write your presentation.

Why traditional 'presentation preparation' doesn't work

The traditional way to prepare a presentation – slide 1, then slide 2, etc. – is totally ineffective. The reason is that, although you are developing arguments in a logical way (a good thing), the presentation gets more interesting as it goes on (Fig. 7.1):

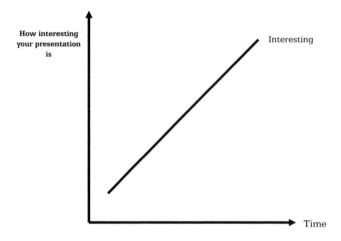

Figure 7.1 'The presentation gets more interesting as it goes on.'

But, as you know, an audience's concentration reduces during a presentation, like in figure 7.2:

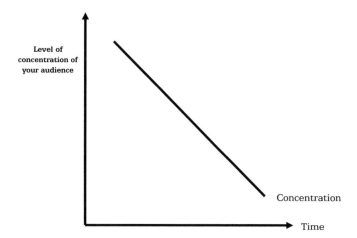

Figure 7.2 'An audience's concentration reduces during a presentation.'

Taking these two graphs together (figure 7.3) shows:

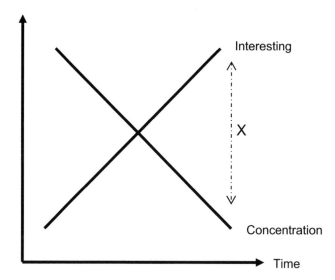

Figure 7.3 As your presentation gets more interesting, the audience's concentration is decreasing.

In other words, you are getting more interesting (Fig. 7.1) as the audience's brain is switching off (Fig. 7.2). So, at point X you're reaching your key points just as they've stopped listening.

The best way to prepare

So, the best way to prepare your presentation is to get your RAP Reminder Card™ and JOLT analysis, and then do the following:

1   Build a skeleton around your 15 seconds

Since your 15 seconds are your most powerful messages, you must base your entire presentation around them.

So create your skeleton by writing your title in a circle in the middle of a page, and drawing a separate branch for each of the points in your 15 seconds (simply copy the wording from your RAP Reminder Card™), like in figure 7.4:

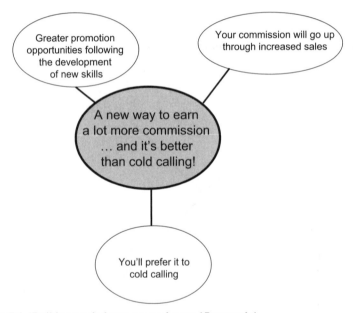

Figure 7.4 'Build your skeleton around your 15 seconds'.

2   Flesh out the skeleton with common sense

Now, on each branch, add *all* the relevant points you can think of to make that branch a compelling argument *for your audience*.

Write *everything* you can think of here. Don't pre-judge if it'll end up in the presentation or not … you'll edit it down later anyway (Fig. 7.5).

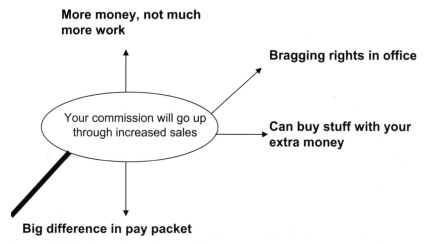

Figure 7.5 'Flesh out the skeleton with common sense.'

For clarity, I am going to show you how this would work with just one of the three branches. Obviously, you would do it with all the branches when preparing your presentation.

3.   Flesh out with 'question words'
You've seen earlier how useful questioning words – who, why, what, etc. – are for developing points. You can use them again here to:

- develop the points you've already got; and
- come up with some new ones (Fig. 7.6).

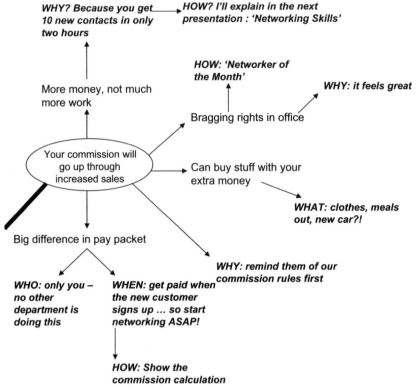

Figure 7.6 'Flesh out with question words.'

4   Flesh out with 'for instance'

A great tip for presentations: *Facts tell; stories sell.*

Personal stories get buy-in from an audience, are memorable and are extremely useful tools for aiding explanations. This being the case, your presentations need stories.

The type, style and duration of your stories will depend on the *results* and *audience* of RAP, i.e. the results you want, and what your audience will buy into. But, presentations will *always* be better if they include stories.

The most memorable stories are either personal or humorous. You already know this to be true. If I were to ask you to recall something you heard recently that moved you, or made you laugh, you'd no doubt be able to do it easily.

But, if you can't find a suitable personal/humorous story, at the very least find an *interesting* one. If you're making a sales pitch and want to tell the story of how you helped Mr Grey, a Widget Maker, save money on his operational costs, it's going to need a more interesting angle. This could be Mr Grey's hobby, how the two of you first met, a funny thing you once did together ... *anything*. Don't exclude Mr Grey's weekend obsession with naked paragliding because you don't think it's relevant to the presentation. If it makes your content more interesting and *memorable* for the audience, include it.

The easiest way to weave stories into a presentation is:

1   state a fact;
2   'for instance ...' (Fig.7.7, overleaf); then
3   your interesting story.

So, you might say: (1) 'We know we can reduce your operating costs because we're experts at it. (2) For instance, (3) one of our clients is a gentleman called Mr Grey, who has a very interesting weekend hobby ...'

Believe it or not, your presentation is nearly done. So far, you have:

- identified your objective;
- found your 15 seconds;
- JOLTed your audience;
- created your skeleton (with a separate branch for each of the key points in your 15 seconds); and
- fleshed out the skeleton with:
  - common sense;
  - questioning words; and
  - 'For instance'/stories.

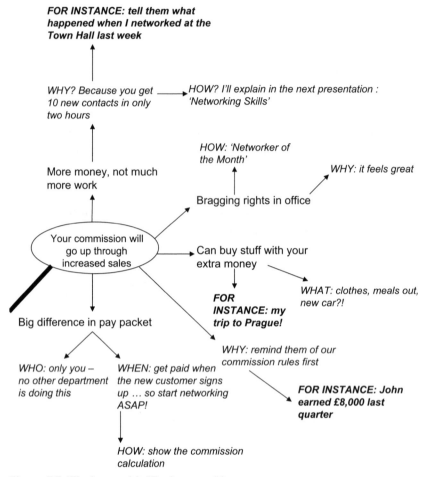

Figure 7.7 'Flesh out with "For instance".'

There are six final steps to completing your presentation. And the first of these is simple, quick and can even be good fun. It's:

5   Cross out the unnecessaries

You now have a very solid skeleton, with lots of flesh on it. But, almost definitely, you'll have *too much* information. You need to un-clutter your presentation by going through *every* point and asking:

'Does this point make me more likely to achieve my objective?'

Your answer will be one of three:

- 'Yes, I must say it'; or
- 'No, I don't need to'; or
- 'I don't need to *say* it, but I should give this info to the audience in a *handout*.' (Fig. 7.8.)

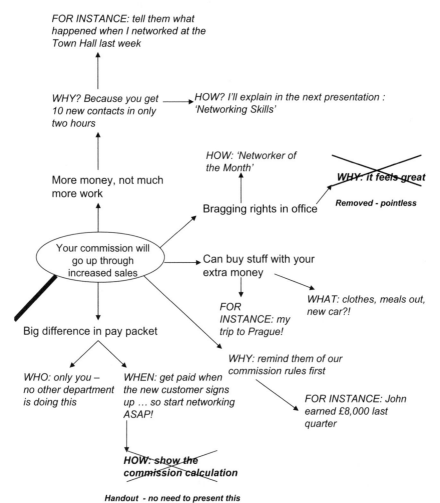

Figure 7.8 'You need to unclutter your presentation.'

6   'If I were you ...'

Your penultimate task in assembling content centres around the fact your audiences will often have their own information, thoughts and preconceptions about your topic, some of which won't be favourable. This could be, in a sales pitch, the potential customer knowing about your competitors' strengths. Or, when you want your colleagues to buy into something, but they see that as extra work for them and don't want to know.

So, how to handle their preconceptions? If you don't address their concerns during your presentation, one of two things will happen:

- the audience could voice these issues in a rabble-rousing way; which quickly gets out of hand; or
- even more worryingly, they don't raise them, so they are never addressed.

Both are disasters. The first is not pleasant and is hard to rectify. The second is an absolute catastrophe, because their negative preconceptions have never been addressed so are still there.

A third option is for you to proactively mention their concerns during your presentation, and address them there and then.

The phrase to introduce these concerns is 'If I were you', followed by the concern(s) *using words they might have said themselves*. This shows total empathy, and that you see it from their point of view.

You then address their concern(s) using *pre-prepared* lines that maximise your chance of eliminating them.

A word of warning here: note the term *pre-prepared*. It is *critical* you prepare this in advance, or you run the risk of jellying, and throwing everything you can think of to address the point. And, of course, the more meandering your explanation, the more your audience, think 'I don't buy this'.

So, address audience concerns in your presentation. Be totally prepared. Totally focussed. Totally succinct. So that you address them quickly, efficiently and then can move on to the rest of your presentation.

Example

'*If I were you*, I'd be thinking "Does this mean I'm going to be working a lot more evenings?"'

'Well, yes, there *is* some evening work to be done, but – as you know – we're very flexible with working hours here. So, if you were to go networking on a Wednesday evening, you could come in late on the Thursday, for example.

'But, don't forget that all of us here are judged by the Board on how many sales we bring in every week. And, being an effective networker is a sure-fire way of impressing the powers-that-be here.

'To me, a few late evenings is a small price to pay for impressing the paymasters.

'Also, as you've seen, networking can happen at any time, from office meetings, to train journeys. It doesn't – indeed, *shouldn't* – just happen during the evening.'

---

7   Call to action

The final piece of the jigsaw is one that very few presenters include, yet it's crucial. Without it, chances of success are slim.

It goes at the end of your presentation. It's your call to action: in other words, crystal clear directions to your audience as to what you want them to do next.

You'll have been to many presentations where, at the end, you've thought, 'Okay, that makes perfect sense. But what am I supposed to do now?'

You don't want your audience thinking this, so you must be very precise as to what you want them to do.

To create your call to action, it's always worth going back to your RAP Reminder Card™ (page 193) to remind yourself what your objective is, then base your call to action on that.

As a final point, notice how the example below starts off with some simple thoughts that the audience can't help but nod in agreement with. Once you start audiences nodding, it's easier to keep them doing so!

The thought process

- I want them to *want* to go networking.
- So, I need a commitment from them that they'll do it.
- But I'm doing skills training later, so don't want them to start networking yet.

Therefore, the call to action (starting the nodding early)

1 'Today's presentation is all about increasing your commission. I take it I'm right that you do want to increase your commission?' [Yes.]
2 'Can you all see that networking could help you achieve this?' [Yes.]
3 'I know you don't know how to network yet – I'll show you that later – but all I need from you now is a commitment that you'll look into it. Do you think it's worth exploring?' [Yes.]
4 'So, I take it you're all happy to go to the next stage, which is to show you how to network effectively?'

---

8   The layout that puts your key points in the audience's long term
     memory

It's nearly time to turn your workings into your presentation. The only remaining question is: what order should you say your content in?

Well, you want your content to be in the order that gives you the best chance of the audience being convinced by – and *remembering* – it.

To show you how an audience's memory works, try this exercise, which I first saw in Tony Buzan's book *Brilliant Memory: Unlock the power of your mind* (1997, Bard Press).

Look down this list of words, and remember as many as you can. Only read the list once. Spend no more than twenty seconds doing so …

Hen

Bus

Brown

Hit

Potato

Seven

Then

Why

Fortune

Then

Toe

Hat

Field

Then

Swim

The Grand Old Duke of York

Never

Then

By

Ever

Blunt

Then

Flute

High

Tar

Horse

Tailor

Now, without looking back, answer the following:

1   What were the first five words?
2   What were the last five words?
3   Which word was repeated?
4   What was the long phrase in the middle of the list?

Look back at the list of words and see how you did. To put your results in context, (and don't worry how you compare with what follows – it tests *memory*, not *intelligence*, after all!), I have performed a version of this exercise on stage to tens of thousands of people in the last couple of years. Three recurring themes for any audience of any size in any country are:

- people tend to do much better on question 1 than question 2;
- most people seem to answer question 3 correctly; and
- practically everybody remembers question 4.

The four ways memories work are shown in figure 7.9:

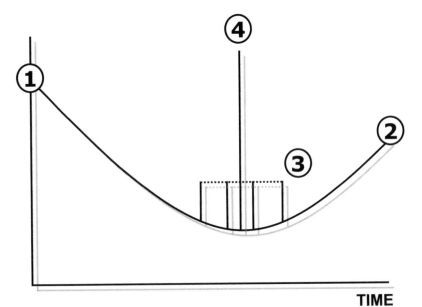

Figure 7.9 The four ways memories work. See Table 7.2 on the next page for an explanation of each reference point.

Graph reference	Memory Bias	Meaning you remember things ...
1	Early Bias	... at the start
2	Recency Bias	... at the end
3	Repetitive Bias	... that are repeated
4	Outstanding Bias	... that stand out in some way

Table 7.2 Explanation of each reference point in figure 7.9

The level to which each individual's memory works varies, but the fact is that everybody remembers things in a combination of these four ways.

And now comes a very important point. Look at these two facts you now know:

- your 15 seconds are the points most likely to help you achieve your objective; and
- each audience member's memory works in some/all of these four ways – first, last, repeated or outstanding.

These two facts lead us to this conclusion:

> To give yourself the best chance of achieving your presentation's objective, you must say *each* of your key points (your 15 seconds) in *each* of the four memory ways.

So, the ideal layout is the one shown in figure 7.10.

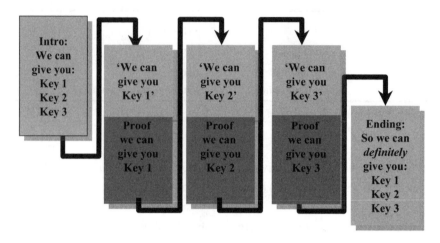

Figure 7.10 The ideal layout for your presentation.

Notice how each of your 15 seconds hits the four long term memory hotspots. They appear at the *start*, at the *end*, are *repeated* and will include an *outstanding* element (because your content for each point will include something that stands out to the audience. Figure 7.11 shows how this would look for this section's example.

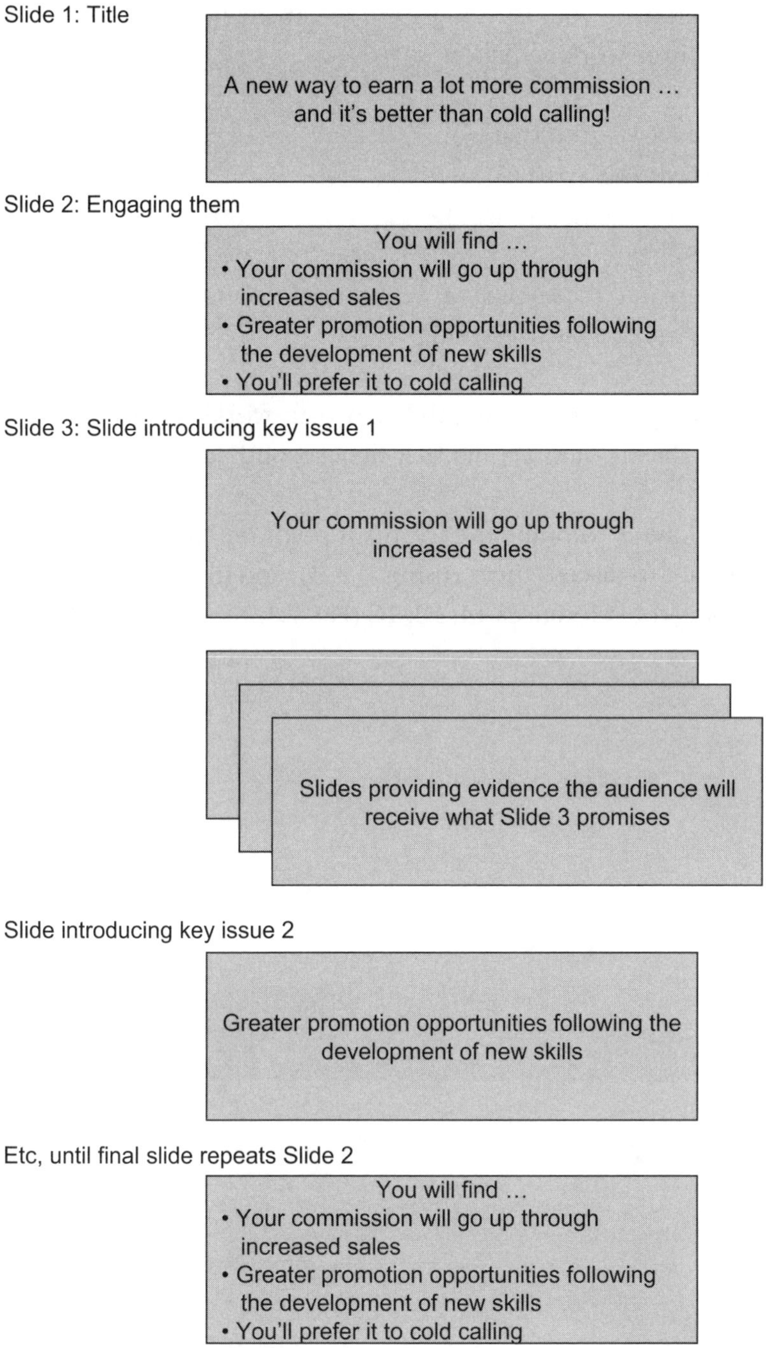

Slide 1: Title

A new way to earn a lot more commission ...
and it's better than cold calling!

Slide 2: Engaging them

You will find ...
• Your commission will go up through
  increased sales
• Greater promotion opportunities following
  the development of new skills
• You'll prefer it to cold calling

Slide 3: Slide introducing key issue 1

Your commission will go up through
increased sales

Slides providing evidence the audience will
receive what Slide 3 promises

Slide introducing key issue 2

Greater promotion opportunities following the
development of new skills

Etc, until final slide repeats Slide 2

You will find ...
• Your commission will go up through
  increased sales
• Greater promotion opportunities following
  the development of new skills
• You'll prefer it to cold calling

Figure 7.11 How the skeleton of the presentation for this example would look.

9   Transferring your workings into the above layout

You have three working papers:

- your big skeleton (part 5);
- 'If I were you' (part 6); and
- your call to action (part 7).

To slot them into the layout you've just read, you have to work out the *order* you want to say everything.

So it's simply a case of going through your workings, and thinking, 'Which of these points should I say first, second?' and so on.

My technique is to number each main point on each branch in the order I want to discuss them (using 1, 2, 3), and then order each sub-point using the references 1A, 1B, 1C (Fig. 7.12).

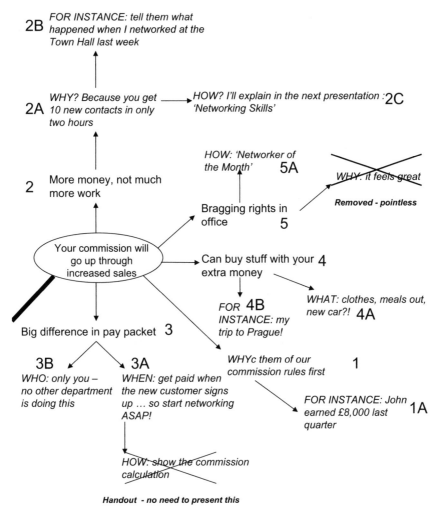

Figure 7.12 'My technique is to number each main point on each branch in the order I want to discuss them (using 1, 2, 3), and then order each sub-point using the references 1A, 1B, 1C.'

I find it then helps me to transfer the ordered workings into a more traditional linear style. At this stage, I also think how I am going to link the points together.

Remind them of our commission rules

(link)For instance
John earned £8,000 last quarter.

So, it's great for increasing your money. But even better ...

It's not much more work

Because
You'll get 10 new contacts in only two hours.

For instance
Tell them what happened at the Town Hall last week.

That sounds great, doesn't it? Don't worry ...
I'll explain how to do it in a later presentation ('Networking Skills').

So, it's not much work, but there could be a ...

Big difference in pay packet

As you know
You get your commission in when the new customer signs up ... so start networking ASAP!

Even better news
Only you – no other department in our firm is doing this.

So, you've got more money. What are you going to do with it?

Can buy stuff with your extra money

You might want
Clothes, meals out, new car, etc.

For instance
My trip to Prague (paid for by last quarter's commission).

> *So, as well as cars and holidays, is there anything else good about what I'm sharing with you today? Well, yes …*
>
> **Bragging rights in office**
>
> *As an incentive*
> 'Networker of the Month'.
>
> *So, you can see networking substantially increases your commission. But it also …*

10   An important point about linking:
Notice the smoothness of the transitions in the above script? You want this with your presentation, so you need good links between points.

The best mechanism for this is what I call *Bye Hi*: say *Bye* to the previous points and *Hi* to the new one.

For example see how the asterisked sentence works in this format 'So, it's great for increasing your money ['Bye' to the previous point (money)], but, even better ['Hi' to the next point]'.

11   Building slides (if you're using them) using the 'Two Ronnies' approach
Have you heard of the phrase 'death by PowerPoint'?

Have you ever been on the receiving end of a presentation that this phrase could have been invented for?!

I have. So many times, it's frightening. One that has stayed with me for years was by someone who'll remain nameless. The 'highlights' were:

- Every slide was crammed with words.
- Every slide looked the same: yellow writing on a blue background.
- The words were so small you couldn't read them.
- There were 136 slides.

- The presentation was one hour long.
- She read every single slide out word for word, adding nothing.
- The worst bit: she'd given us copies of the slides in advance, so we could read ahead.

It was *dire*. As I write this, I remember the utter helplessness that I felt after two minutes, knowing exactly what the next 58 minutes had in store for me … and that there was *nothing* I could do about it.

To make sure your slides don't have this effect, think of you and them as a double act.

You will notice the title to this section makes reference to the 'Two Ronnies', who were a famous British comedy act – Ronnie Barker and Ronnie Corbett. Their shows were the usual mix of jokes, sketches and the like.

One format for their jokes was a mock news show, where they would introduce jokes by saying, 'And in the news today …', and follow it with a funny story.

When they were reading out the news, they always spoke alternately. One Ronnie would tell a joke; then the other would tell the next joke. You never saw *both* Ronnies saying the *same* joke at the *same* time. If they had done this, you would have shouted at the television: 'Will one of you two Ronnies SHUT UP! I can't understand a word, when you're both saying the same thing at the same time.'

It's the same with your slides. When you're presenting, you're Ronnie One; your slides, Ronnie Two.

And you don't want your audience shouting, 'Will one of you two Ronnies SHUT UP! I can't understand a word, when you're both saying the same thing at the same time.'

You see, you (Ronnie One) are really good at certain things. You can engage people. Discuss topics in full sentences. Speak with passion on your subject. Interact with the audience, engage with them. Inject personality.

But the slideshow (Ronnie Two) is brilliant at other things. He is very good at showing images, graphics, diagrams, charts, graphs, etc.

It wouldn't make sense for you (Ronnie One) to verbally describe a six-segment pie chart, when Ronnie Two could simply hold it up on a slide. Similarly it doesn't make sense for Ronnie Two to say full sentences, because slides aren't very good at injecting passion into lots of words. That's your job.

If you like, think of yourself as the *Passion Ronnie*, and the slides as the *Picture Ronnie*. You have to present so that both of you are maximising your relative strengths. Lots of words on slides is not playing to his strength. And it is this which is so prevalent in the business world today, and has led to the phrase 'death by PowerPoint'.

Following the logic here, if the two Ronnies aren't both speaking at the same time, that suggests neither are saying the full message. And that's right. A presentation needs *both* of you. So, your slides *must not make sense on their own*. If they do, Ronnie Two is saying the whole message. There is no need for Ronnie One. In fact, if your slides are that verbose, I wouldn't bother presenting them. I'd simply email them to the audience, and ask them to call if they have any questions.

As well as reducing words and increasing visuals on the slides, there are two final points to remember with slides:

- If you put all the information on a slide so it appears all at once, the audience will read ahead. You know this to be case. Think of the last presentation you saw when five pullet points came up at once. The presenter waxed lyrically about point 1, whilst you read points 2–5 and then wanted him to click to the next slide. So, always build the slides up as you go through them.

- The most important function of PowerPoint is the letter B. Press B on the keyboard and it blanks the PowerPoint screen. This means that you can shut Ronnie Two up while you're talking, so the audience isn't looking at him, but focusing their sole attention on you.

Practise, practise, practise

> A music student once went up to famed violinist, Fritz Kreisler, and said to him 'I'd give up my whole life to play as beautifully as you just did.'
>
> To which Mr Kreisler replied: 'I did.'

Your presentation is now complete. But it's 100% definitely *not* going to work if you don't deliver it well.

So you need to practise. And the more you practise, the more you know the material, and the better you get.

The traditional approach to practising is shown in figure 7.13 (assume the ten boxes represent slides, and that the grey shading shows where people traditionally focus their attention when practising – the darker the grey, the more intense the practice):

Figure 7.13 Traditionally, people focus their attention more on earlier slides than later ones.

Do you recognise this? This method of practising is often closely followed by the presenter running out of time, so her or she has to 'wing it' anyway.

Although there is a lot of logic in starting at the beginning when prac-tising, there are some serious problems, including:

- the ending – which, as you know, is *critical* – is often too weak because it's not been practised;
- the links are not seamless, so the presentation is disjointed;
- you are focusing your practice on the wrong part. You know your topic fairly well anyway, so why spend so much time practising the slides' content? Spend more time on the *Bye Hi* links.

Instead, a much better way to practise a presentation is that shown in figure 7.14:

Figure 7.14 'Practise the start, end and links until they all become second nature; then, do one or two full run-throughs, spending extra time on tricky bits.'

So, practise the start, end and links until they all become second nature; then, do one or two full run-throughs, spending extra time on tricky bits, like the *If I were you* section, page 206.

This approach is much better. Your presentation will have more cohe-sion. You get to the end more quickly. And you are practising the areas where you are most likely to become unstuck – the start, the end and the linking of topics.

A further word of warning here when practising: however long the presentation takes when practising in your bedroom, it will take at least 25% longer on the day. You will probably ad lib more, there will be questions, etc. … So, if you've been given 25 minutes to present, make sure it only takes 20 minutes when practising …

During – delivery skills to impress your audience

Presentation delivery skills are a subject in their own right. You could write a whole book on it. In fact, countless thousands of authors have done.

Because this book is all about reducing your jelly, the thrust of this chapter is about producing audience-friendly, jelly-free content that gives you the maximum chance of achieving your objective.

However, I think it would be inappropriate of me to exclude delivery skills entirely from a section on presentations. After all, *if I were you*, I would want some simple hints I could apply straight away to improve my delivery.

Figures 7.15 and 7.16 give another excerpt from my sales programme *Win That Pitch: A Step by Step Guide to Winning More Business* (www. andybounds.com/winthatpitch). It contains some really simple tips on body language that will make a big difference to your effectiveness on the day …

12.4 Default positions

"...you need to have default positions for your hands, feet, chin, head and eyes."

To maximise the power of your body language, you need to have default positions for your hands, feet, chin, head and eyes. Confused? Let me explain...

A) Hands

Well, for hands, a question I'm frequently asked is "what do I do with my hands?"

Presenters often worry about their hands – they're overly conscious of them when they present.

Are you like this? If so, the solution is simple: find your default position.

Work out where your hands will be when they are not moving, and then always bring them back to here once you've stopped moving them.

My hands' default position is 'praying' – palms together, around waist height. I separate them when I'm making a point, but they come back together after that.

Find your hands' default position – it's a huge relief when you do.

B) Feet

"...put 60% of your body weight on the balls of your feet; and 40% on the heels.."

For your feet, don't roam around aimlessly. Nor sway. Nor wander back and forth.

Instead, when you're standing, have your feet 2 to 3 inches wider apart than you normally would, and put 60% of your body weight on the balls of your feet; and 40% on the heels. It might be worth standing up now and trying it before you move on?

This default position for your feet gives you good balance, minimises the risk of swaying, and moving aimlessly about.

But what about moving about? What if you want to?

I would move, to be honest. It adds to the energy the audience sees. It's also a good way of dispelling any butterflies you might be feeling. Try it – and watch your butterflies reduce.

How you move is key though. Don't wander slowly. Don't lollop around.

Figure 7.15 *Win that Pitch* module 12, page 16. www.andybounds.com/winthatpitch

Instead, fix on a spot 2 to 3 paces away that you want to stand on. And walk purposefully – with certainty and energy – towards it.

When you get there, re–route yourself with legs apart, 60% of the weight on the balls of your feet etc. as before.

C) Chin

"There should be a parallel imaginary line between your two chins too."

Your head angle betrays all sorts of emotions.

If your head is looking upwards with your chin pointing upwards, you come across as aloof. If your head is dipped slightly and your chin is pointing down, you look slightly nervous. And if your chin is pointing right down at the floor, you can look downright evil!

So, your chin's default position should be as follows:

Imagine a line going from your eyes to your audience members' eyes. There should be a parallel imaginary line between your two chins too. If there is, your head angle is correct, and transmitting the messages you want it to.

D) Head

As a child you have been told many times to "stand up straight".

And it is as relevant now as it ever was.

"The taller you stand, the straighter your back, the more certainty you transmit."

The taller you stand, the straighter your back, the more certainty you transmit. The more power you have as a speaker. And the more buyable from you are.

E) Eyes

Look at theirs.

If you're nervous, you can probably look at their 3rd eye (it's on their forehead) and they won't even notice. But eye contact is critical, as you know.

Make sure you do it.

Figure 7.16 *Win that Pitch* module 12, page 17. www.andybounds.com/winthat-pitch

After – how to follow up your presentation, to ensure you get great results

Picture the scene.

Everything has gone brilliantly so far. You prepared your presentation in the right way. You delivered it like a pro. At the end of the presentation, the audience said 'yes'. Everything has gone as planned.

Unfortunately, there is still an area where many presentations are won and lost. And that's in the follow-up.

Even if you get a 'yes' from the audience on the day, it's still your responsibility to ensure that this 'yes' translates to actual achievement of your objective.

For instance, if you are making a sales pitch, it's not enough for the prospective customer to say, 'Yes, we'll buy from you'. You need them to actually sign the order form.

So, it is important to follow up. I am sure there's been many a time when you felt your audience said 'yes', but then nothing happened. And it is *so frustrating*.

To follow up, it's a question of getting *agreement*:

- *agreement* from them on your call to action; and
- *agreement* on *who* will do *what* and *when*.

> 'Great stuff. So we're all agreed then. To take this forward, I'll send you an email detailing when the networking skills course will take place. You'll get this by the end of today. I'll need you to confirm attendance, book it in your diary and then we can get things moving. Is that OK?'

How to use this section to create presentations that work

Follow the advice in this section, and you will create a jelly-free presentation that *works*. It will contain only the information you *need* to say. And that information will be phrased such that audiences will buy into it.

However, the next time you have a presentation to do, you don't want to be wading through this entire section from beginning to end again. To use this chapter as a guideline for future presentations:

1   read the worked example only;
2   prepare your presentation in the same style; and
3   only go back to the rest of the chapter if you need more detail.

This style of presentation is very powerful. I have used it time and time again, for companies in all types of industries, all over the world. And it *works*.

Do you remember my question earlier in this section: how do you prepare – in a blind panic, by making minor tweaks to an existing presentation, or a bit of both? Well, once you have prepared a presentation using the techniques in this section, you'll never do either of these ever again!

Avoiding 'the Green Corridor of Doom'

8

🔖

THE STORY SO FAR …

You now know that you can only gauge whether communication is effective or not by what happens AFTER it.

But, AFTERs are also relevant to business books. Because a business book is only effective if the reader's skills develop AFTER reading it.

So will this book help *your* skills develop? Will it help you communicate better? Will you have more productive meetings? Better sales appointments? Give better presentations?

Or might you end up in 'the green corridor of doom' …

THE GREEN CORRIDOR OF DOOM

I remember when my first child, Megan, was born. I thought I was the *best Dad ever*. Because she was just so *happy.* She loved everyone, she was perfectly behaved, anyone could ask her to do *anything* and she'd do it.

I was the first of my friends to have a child and they'd often say, 'Boundsy, you're brilliant at being a Dad'.

I knew I'd found my vocation in life. After all, it was just so easy being a Dad.

And.

Then.

Came.

Jack.

Is it just me, or do little boys just *not* do what they're told?

He was always messing about, up to mischief. Never remotely coming close to doing what I asked him to.

And then it suddenly dawned on me ... I was not the *best Dad ever*. It was just that Megan had been the *best baby ever*!

But, as I got to know Jack, I realised he wasn't naughty. He wasn't seeking to disobey me. It's just that he would literally forget what I had just told him, because he'd found something more interesting to focus on instead. This became really apparent to me when, one evening, I asked him to get his tractor book ...

This book was Jack's favourite book as a toddler. I must have read it to him over ten thousand times. Every time I suggested I read it he'd get really excited. This time was no different ...

He and I were in the lounge at the time, which was located at the end of a long corridor. In fact, the flat where we lived then was basically one very long corridor with all the rooms leading off it. The corridor had green carpet, and green walls. We called it 'the green corridor'. And the lounge was at one end, Jack's bedroom at the other.

I clearly remember Jack setting off down the corridor singing to himself, 'Tractor book, tractor book … I'm getting my tractor book.' I can still picture watching his back as he walked down the corridor, thinking how much I loved my son, and how sweet he was.

But then, half way down the corridor, he stopped suddenly, looked at the doorway he was standing next to, shouted the word 'bathroom', and ran through it.

Unbelievable. Distracted again. He was about to read his favourite book. He *only* had to get to the end of the corridor. But something more interesting had come up.

I raced down the green corridor, went into the bathroom, and found Jack sitting on the floor. I said to him, 'Jack, what are you doing?'

'Playing, Dad.'

'But what about your tractor book?'

'What tractor book?'

He had totally forgotten. Couldn't remember at all. Even though sitting on his Dad's knee to hear his tractor book was his favourite thing, it had gone completely from his mind.

And, as I think of Jack and his tractor book, it makes me think of how most people are when reading business books. They read something they like, something that will help their business grow. Something they want to implement – say, the AFTERs. And then they start off down the green corridor of doom …

Instead of singing 'tractor book, tractor book', they think 'AFTERs, AFTERs'.

But – just like Jack and the bathroom – halfway down the green corridor of doom, something distracts them. It could be anything, from an urgent deadline, to reading emails. And if I were to come running down the green corridor after them and say, 'What are you doing?', they would reply, 'Reading emails'.

'But what about the AFTERs?'

And, just like Jack, they would respond: 'What AFTERs? Oh them … I'll get round to them in a minute … just after I do this …'

So, how can you make sure *you* don't disappear down the green corridor of doom …?

HOW THIS BOOK CAN HELP YOU GROW YOUR BUSINESS

It would be hugely hypocritical of me to write a book extolling the virtues of AFTERs if my book wasn't geared to helping your business AFTER reading it. So, here are four simple steps to ensure you make the most of everything you've read:

1 Look through the summaries at the start of each section.
2 To remind yourself of the detail on any of them, skim-read the relevant section(s).
3 Think which bit(s) of the book you want to implement in your business first, and give it a go …
4 NEVER JELLY ANYONE AGAIN!

And if you want even more help ...

HOW ANDY BOUNDS CAN HELP YOU FURTHER

Andy Bounds can improve your organisation's communication, by showing you what to say so audiences engage with, buy into and – most importantly – *act* on your content.

You can book Andy to speak at your conferences and team events, or to coach your senior decision makers. His areas of expertise include:

- Improving your communication;
- Employee engagement;
- What to say so others buy into you, and your words;
- Sell more by saying less;
- How to get thunderous applause after every presentation you give;
- Win that sales pitch;
- Get paid what you're worth;
- Charismatic presenting skills;
- Preparing for important presentations quickly and effectively; and
- How to increase your referral business.

To book Andy, or one of his team, contact:

- telephone: +44 (0) 800 781 3799
- email: office@andybounds.com
- website: www.andybounds.com

Win That Pitch: a step by step guide to winning more business
Andy has created his own sales programme that will help you win more business.

Described by former UK Entrepreneur of the Year, Steve Pipe, as: '... without doubt the most concise, brilliantly structured and simple selling process I have ever come across', *Win That Pitch* gives you a simple structure to follow to create your own sales pitch. Simply do the exercises in the programme and, as you turn the final page, you'll have your new sales pitch written. A pitch that will help you win more business.

You can buy *Win That Pitch* now by visiting www.andybounds.com/winthatpitch

INDEX